MOS 2016 Study Guide for Microsoft Excel

Joan E. Lambert

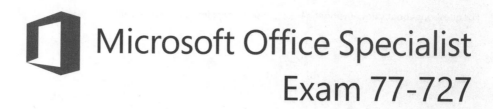

Microsoft Office Specialist
Exam 77-727

MOS 2016 Study Guide for Microsoft Excel

Published with the authorization of Microsoft Corporation by:
Pearson Education, Inc.

ISBN-13: 978-0-7356-9943-4
ISBN-10: 0-7356-9943-7

Library of Congress Control Number: 2016953071

4 18

For information about buying this title in bulk quantities, or for special sales opportunities (which may include electronic versions; custom cover designs; and content particular to your business, training goals, marketing focus, or branding interests), please contact our corporate sales department at corpsales@pearsoned.com or (800) 382-3419.

For government sales inquiries, please contact governmentsales@pearsoned.com.

For questions about sales outside the U.S., please contact intlcs@pearson.com.

Editor-in-Chief
Greg Wiegand

Senior Acquisitions Editor
Laura Norman

Senior Production Editor
Tracey Croom

Editorial Production
Online Training Solutions, Inc.
(OTSI)

Series Project Editor
Kathy Krause (OTSI)

Indexer
Susie Carr (OTSI)

Copy Editor/Proofreader
Jaime Odell (OTSI)

Editorial Assistant
Cindy J. Teeters

Interior Designer/Compositor
Joan Lambert (OTSI)

Cover Designer
Twist Creative • Seattle

Contents

What do you think of this book? We want to hear from you!

Microsoft is interested in hearing your feedback so we can improve our books and learning resources for you. To participate in a brief survey, please visit:

https://aka.ms/tellpress

3   Create tables   99

4   Perform operations with formulas and functions   119

What do you think of this book? We want to hear from you!

Microsoft is interested in hearing your feedback so we can improve our books and learning resources for you. To participate in a brief survey, please visit:

https://aka.ms/tellpress

Introduction

The Microsoft Office Specialist (MOS) certification program has been designed to validate your knowledge of and ability to use programs in the Microsoft Office 2016 suite of programs. This book has been designed to guide you in studying the types of tasks you are likely to be required to demonstrate in Exam 77-727: Microsoft Excel 2016.

See Also For information about the tasks you are likely to be required to demonstrate in Exam 77-728: Microsoft Excel 2016 Expert, see *MOS 2016 Study Guide for Microsoft Excel Expert* by Paul McFedries (Microsoft Press, 2017).

Who this book is for

MOS 2016 Study Guide for Microsoft Excel is designed for experienced computer users seeking Microsoft Office Specialist certification in Excel 2016.

MOS exams for individual programs are practical rather than theoretical. You must demonstrate that you can complete certain tasks or projects rather than simply answer questions about program features. The successful MOS certification candidate will have at least six months of experience using all aspects of the application on a regular basis; for example, using Excel at work or school to create and manage workbooks and worksheets, modify and format cell content, summarize and organize data, present data in tables and charts, perform data operations by using functions and formulas, and insert and format objects on worksheets.

As a certification candidate, you probably have a lot of experience with the program you want to become certified in. Many of the procedures described in this book will be familiar to you; others might not be. Read through each study section and ensure that you are familiar with the procedures, concepts, and tools discussed. In some cases, images depict the tools you will use to perform procedures related to the skill set. Study the images and ensure that you are familiar with the options available for each tool.

How this book is organized

The exam coverage is divided into chapters representing broad skill sets that correlate to the functional groups covered by the exam. Each chapter is divided into sections addressing groups of related skills that correlate to the exam objectives. Each section includes review information, generic procedures, and practice tasks you can complete on your own while studying. We provide practice files you can use to work through the practice tasks, and results files you can use to check your work. You can practice the generic procedures in this book by using the practice files supplied or by using your own files.

Throughout this book, you will find Exam Strategy tips that present information about the scope of study that is necessary to ensure that you achieve mastery of a skill set and are successful in your certification effort.

Download the practice files

Before you can complete the practice tasks in this book, you need to copy the book's practice files and results files to your computer. Download the compressed (zipped) folder from the following page, and extract the files from it to a folder (such as your Documents folder) on your computer:

https://aka.ms/MOSExcel2016/downloads

IMPORTANT The Excel 2016 program is not available from this website. You should purchase and install that program before using this book.

You will save the completed versions of practice files that you modify while working through the practice tasks in this book. If you later want to repeat the practice tasks, you can download the original practice files again.

The following table lists the practice files provided for this book.

Folder and objective group	Practice files	Result files
MOSExcel2016\Objective1 Create and manage worksheets and workbooks	Excel_1-1.xlsx	Excel_1-1_Results subfolder: ■ Excel_1-1_results.xlsx ■ MyBlank_results.xlsx ■ MyCalc_results.xlsx
	Excel_1-2.xlsx	Excel_1-2_results.xlsx
	Excel_1-3.xlsx	Excel_1-3_results.xlsx
	Excel_1-4.xlsx	Excel_1-4_results.xlsx
	Excel_1-5.xlsx	Excel_1-5_Results subfolder: ■ Excel_1-5a_results.xlsx ■ MOS-Compatible.xls ■ MOS-Template.xltm
MOSExcel2016\Objective2 Manage data cells and ranges	Excel_2-1.xlsx	Excel_2-1_results.xlsx
	Excel_2-2.xlsx	Excel_2-2_results.xlsx
	Excel_2-3.xlsx	Excel_2-3_results.xlsx
MOSExcel2016\Objective3 Create tables	Excel_3-1.xlsx	Excel_3-1_results.xlsx
	Excel_3-2.xlsx	Excel_3-2_results.xlsx
	Excel_3-3.xlsx	Excel_3-3_results.xlsx
MOSExcel2016\Objective4 Perform operations with formulas and functions	Excel_4-1a.xlsx	Excel_4-1a_results.xlsx
	Excel_4-1b.xlsx	Excel_4-1b_results.xlsx
	Excel_4-1c.xlsx	Excel_4-1c_results.xlsx
	Excel_4-2.xlsx	Excel_4-2_results.xlsx
	Excel_4-3.xlsx	Excel_4-3_results.xlsx
MOSExcel2016\Objective5 Create charts and objects	Excel_5-1.xlsx	Excel_5-1_results.xlsx
	Excel_5-2.xlsx	Excel_5-2_results.xlsx
	Excel_5-3a.xlsx	Excel_5-3_results.xlsx
	Excel_5-3b.jpg	
	Excel_5-3c.txt	

Adapt procedure steps

This book contains many images of user interface elements that you'll work with while performing tasks in Excel on a Windows computer. Depending on your screen resolution or app window width, the Excel ribbon on your screen might look different from that shown in this book. (If you turn on Touch mode, the ribbon displays significantly fewer commands than in Mouse mode.) As a result, procedural instructions that involve the ribbon might require a little adaptation.

Simple procedural instructions use this format:

→ On the **Insert** tab, in the **Illustrations** group, click the **Chart** button.

If the command is in a list, our instructions use this format:

→ On the **Home** tab, in the **Editing** group, click the **Find** arrow and then, in the **Find** list, click **Go To**.

If differences between your display settings and ours cause a button to appear differently on your screen than it does in this book, you can easily adapt the steps to locate the command. First click the specified tab, and then locate the specified group. If a group has been collapsed into a group list or under a group button, click the list or button to display the group's commands. If you can't immediately identify the button you want, point to likely candidates to display their names in ScreenTips.

The instructions in this book assume that you're interacting with on-screen elements on your computer by clicking (with a mouse, touchpad, or other hardware device). If you're using a different method—for example, if your computer has a touchscreen interface and you're tapping the screen (with your finger or a stylus)—substitute the applicable tapping action when you interact with a user interface element.

Instructions in this book refer to user interface elements that you click or tap on the screen as *buttons*, and to physical buttons that you press on a keyboard as *keys*, to conform to the standard terminology used in documentation for these products.

Ebook edition

If you're reading the ebook edition of this book, you can do the following:

- Search the full text
- Print
- Copy and paste

You can purchase and download the ebook edition from the Microsoft Press Store at:

https://aka.ms/MOSExcel2016/detail

Errata, updates, & book support

We've made every effort to ensure the accuracy of this book and its companion content. If you discover an error, please submit it to us through the link at:

https://aka.ms/MOSExcel2016/errata

If you need to contact the Microsoft Press Book Support team, please send an email message to:

mspinput@microsoft.com

For help with Microsoft software and hardware, go to:

https://support.microsoft.com

We want to hear from you

At Microsoft Press, your satisfaction is our top priority, and your feedback our most valuable asset. Please tell us what you think of this book by completing the survey at:

https://aka.ms/tellpress

The survey is short, and we read every one of your comments and ideas. Thanks in advance for your input!

Stay in touch

Let's keep the conversation going! We're on Twitter at:

https://twitter.com/MicrosoftPress

Taking a Microsoft Office Specialist exam

Desktop computing proficiency is increasingly important in today's business world. When screening, hiring, and training employees, employers can feel reassured by relying on the objectivity and consistency of technology certification to ensure the competence of their workforce. As an employee or job seeker, you can use technology certification to prove that you already have the skills you need to succeed, saving current and future employers the time and expense of training you.

Microsoft Office Specialist certification

Microsoft Office Specialist certification is designed to assist students and information workers in validating their skills with Office programs. The following certification paths are available:

- A Microsoft Office Specialist (MOS) is an individual who has demonstrated proficiency by passing a certification exam in one or more Office programs, including Microsoft Word, Excel, PowerPoint, Outlook, or Access.

- A Microsoft Office Specialist Expert (MOS Expert) is an individual who has taken his or her knowledge of Office to the next level and has demonstrated by passing two certification exams that he or she has mastered the more advanced features of Word or Excel.

- A Microsoft Office Specialist Master (MOS Master) is an individual who has demonstrated a broader knowledge of Office skills by passing the Word and Word Expert exams, the Excel and Excel Expert exams, and the PowerPoint, Access, or Outlook exam.

Selecting a certification path

When deciding which certifications you would like to pursue, assess the following:

- The program and program version(s) with which you are familiar
- The length of time you have used the program and how frequently you use it

- Whether you have had formal or informal training in the use of that program

- Whether you use most or all of the available program features

- Whether you are considered a go-to resource by business associates, friends, and family members who have difficulty with the program

Candidates for MOS Expert and MOS Master certification are expected to successfully complete a wide range of standard business tasks. Successful candidates generally have six or more months of experience with the specific Office program, including either formal, instructor-led training or self-study using MOS-approved books, guides, or interactive computer-based materials.

Candidates for MOS Expert and MOS Master certification are expected to successfully complete more complex tasks that involve using the advanced functionality of the program. Successful candidates generally have at least six months, and might have several years, of experience with the programs, including formal, instructor-led training or self-study using MOS-approved materials.

Test-taking tips

Every MOS certification exam is developed from a set of exam skill standards (referred to as the *objective domain*) that are derived from studies of how the Office programs are used in the workplace. Because these skill standards dictate the scope of each exam, they provide critical information about how to prepare for certification. This book follows the structure of the published exam objectives.

See Also For more information about the book structure, see "How this book is organized" in the Introduction.

The MOS certification exams are performance based and require you to complete business-related tasks in the program for which you are seeking certification. For example, you might be presented with a document and told to insert and format additional document elements. Your score on the exam reflects how many of the requested tasks you complete within the allotted time.

Here is some helpful information about taking the exam:

- Keep track of the time. Your exam time does not officially begin until after you finish reading the instructions provided at the beginning of the exam. During the exam, the amount of time remaining is shown in the exam instruction window. You can't pause the exam after you start it.

- Pace yourself. At the beginning of the exam, you will receive information about the tasks that are included in the exam. During the exam, the number of completed and remaining tasks is shown in the exam instruction window.

- Read the exam instructions carefully before beginning. Follow all the instructions provided completely and accurately.

- If you have difficulty performing a task, you can restart it without affecting the result of any completed tasks, or you can skip the task and come back to it after you finish the other tasks on the exam.

- Enter requested information as it appears in the instructions, but without duplicating the formatting unless you are specifically instructed to do so. For example, the text and values you are asked to enter might appear in the instructions in bold and underlined text, but you should enter the information without applying these formats.

- Close all dialog boxes before proceeding to the next exam item unless you are specifically instructed not to do so.

- Don't close task panes before proceeding to the next exam item unless you are specifically instructed to do so.

- If you are asked to print a document, worksheet, chart, report, or slide, perform the task, but be aware that nothing will actually be printed.

- Don't worry about extra keystrokes or mouse clicks. Your work is scored based on its result, not on the method you use to achieve that result (unless a specific method is indicated in the instructions).

- If a computer problem occurs during the exam (for example, if the exam does not respond or the mouse no longer functions) or if a power outage occurs, contact a testing center administrator immediately. The administrator will restart the computer and return the exam to the point where the interruption occurred, with your score intact.

◇◇◇

Exam Strategy This book includes special tips for effectively studying for the Microsoft Office Specialist exams in Exam Strategy paragraphs such as this one.

◇◇◇

Certification benefits

At the conclusion of the exam, you will receive a score report, indicating whether you passed the exam. If your score meets or exceeds the passing standard (the minimum required score), you will be contacted by email by the Microsoft Certification Program team. The email message you receive will include your Microsoft Certification ID and links to online resources, including the Microsoft Certified Professional site. On this site, you can download or order a printed certificate, create a virtual business card, order an ID card, review and share your certification transcript, access the Logo Builder, and access other useful and interesting resources, including special offers from Microsoft and affiliated companies.

Depending on the level of certification you achieve, you will qualify to display one of three logos on your business card and other personal promotional materials. These logos attest to the fact that you are proficient in the applications or cross-application skills necessary to achieve the certification. Using the Logo Builder, you can create a personalized certification logo that includes the MOS logo and the specific programs in which you have achieved certification. If you achieve MOS certification in multiple programs, you can include multiple certifications in one logo.

For more information

To learn more about the Microsoft Office Specialist exams and related courseware, visit:

http://www.certiport.com/mos

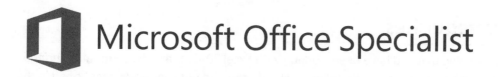

Microsoft Office Specialist

Exam 77-727

Microsoft Excel 2016

This book covers the skills you need to have for certification as a Microsoft Office Specialist in Excel 2016. Specifically, you need to be able to complete tasks that demonstrate the following skill sets:

1   Create and manage worksheets and workbooks
2   Manage data cells and ranges
3   Create tables
4   Perform operations with formulas and functions
5   Create charts and objects

With these skills, you can create and populate Excel workbooks, and format, organize, and present the types of data most commonly used in a business environment.

1

Prerequisites

We assume that you have been working with Excel 2016 for at least six months and that you know how to carry out fundamental tasks that are not specifically mentioned in the objectives for this Microsoft Office Specialist exam. Before you begin studying for this exam, you might want to make sure you are familiar with the information in this section.

Select content

To select all the content in a worksheet

→ At the junction of the row and column headings (above row 1 and to the left of column A), click the **Select All** button.

To select an individual worksheet column or row

→ Click the column heading (labeled with the column letter) or the row heading (labeled with the row number).

To select data in a table, table column, or table row

→ Point to the upper-left corner of the table. When the pointer changes to a diagonal arrow, click once to select only the data, or twice to select the data and headers.

> **Tip** This method works only with tables, not with data ranges.

→ Point to the top edge of the table column. When the pointer changes to a downward-pointing arrow, click once to select only the data, or twice to select the data and header.

> **Tip** You must point to the edge of the table, not to the column heading or row heading.

→ Point to the left edge of the table row. When the pointer changes to a right-pointing arrow, click once to select the data.

Manage data entry

You enter text or a number in a cell simply by clicking the cell and entering the content. When entering content, a Cancel button (an X) and an Enter button (a check mark) are located between the formula bar and Name box, and the indicator at the left end of the status bar changes from Ready to Enter.

Excel allows a long text entry to overflow into an adjacent empty cell and truncates the entry only if the adjacent cell also contains an entry. However, unless you tell it otherwise, Excel displays long numbers in their simplest form, as follows:

- If you enter a number with fewer than 12 digits in a standard-width cell (which holds 8.43 characters), Excel adjusts the width of the column to accommodate the entry.

- If you enter a number with 12 or more digits, Excel displays it in scientific notation. For example, if you enter 12345678912345 in a standard-width cell, Excel displays 1.23457E+13 (1.23457 times 10 to the thirteenth power).

- If you enter a value with many decimal places, Excel might round it. For example, if you enter 123456.789 in a standard-width cell, Excel displays 123456.8.

- If you manually set the width of a column and then enter a numeric value that is too large to be displayed in its entirety, Excel displays pound signs (#) instead of the value.

To complete data entry

→ Click the **Enter** button (the check mark) on the formula bar to complete the entry and stay in the same cell.

→ Press **Enter** or the **Down Arrow** key to complete the entry and move down to the next cell in the same column.

→ Press the **Tab** key or the **Right Arrow** key to complete the entry and move (to the right) to the next cell in the same row, or to the next cell in the table (which might be the first cell of the next row).

→ Press **Shift+Enter** or the **Up Arrow** key to complete the entry and move up to the previous cell in the same column.

→ Press **Shift+Tab** or the **Left Arrow** key to complete the entry and move (to the left) to the previous cell in the same row.

Manage worksheets

To delete a worksheet

→ Right-click the worksheet tab, and then click **Delete**.

→ With the worksheet active, on the **Home** tab, in the **Cells** group, click the **Delete** arrow, and then click **Delete Sheet**.

Reuse content

Excel offers several methods of cutting and copying content. After selecting the content, you can click buttons on the ribbon, use a keyboard shortcut, or right-click the selection and click commands on the shortcut menu. Cutting or copying content places it on the Microsoft Office Clipboard, which is shared by Excel and other Office programs such as Word and PowerPoint. You can paste content that is stored on the Clipboard into a workbook (or any Office file) by using commands from the ribbon, shortcut menu, or keyboard, or directly from the Clipboard.

Experienced users might find it fastest to use a keyboard shortcut. The main keyboard shortcuts for editing tasks are shown in the following table.

Task	Keyboard shortcut
Cut	Ctrl+X
Copy	Ctrl+C
Paste	Ctrl+V
Undo	Ctrl+Z
Repeat/Redo	Ctrl+Y

Exam Strategy When you paste content onto an Excel worksheet, the Paste Options menu presents options for formatting the pasted content. Exam 77-727 requires that you demonstrate the ability to use common paste options, including pasting values, pasting without formatting, and transposing data.

Excel shares the Office Clipboard with Word and other programs in the Microsoft Office suite of products. You can easily reuse content from one Office file in another.

To paste cells from the Clipboard to a data range

1. Select the upper-left cell of the area into which you want to insert the cut or copied cells.

2. On the **Home** tab, in the **Cells** group, click the **Insert** arrow, and then click **Insert Cut Cells** or **Insert Copied Cells**.

3. In the **Insert Paste** dialog box, click **Shift cells right** or **Shift cells down** to move the existing data. Then click **OK**.

To paste cells from the Clipboard over existing data

1. Select the upper-left cell of the area into which you want to insert the cut or copied cells.

2. Do either of the following:

    - On the **Home** tab, in the **Clipboard** group, click **Paste**.

    - Press **Ctrl+V**.

Access program commands and options

Commands for working with Excel workbooks (rather than worksheet content) are available from the Backstage view. You display the Backstage view by clicking the File tab on the ribbon.

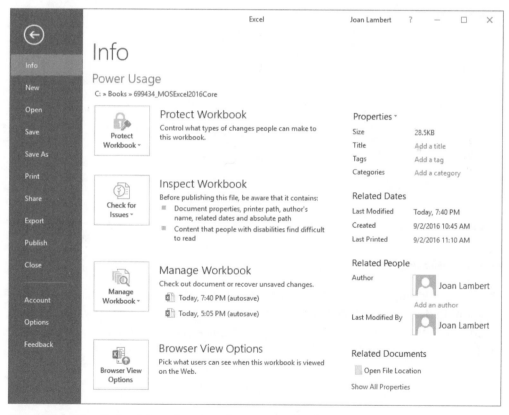

The Backstage view displays information about the current workbook

The links in the left pane of the Backstage view provide access to 11 pages that contain information about the current workbook, commands for working with the workbook or active worksheet, or commands for working with Excel. To display the Info, New, Open, Save As, History, Print, Share, Export, Account, Options, or Feedback page, click the page name in the left pane.

You manage many aspects of Excel functionality from the Excel Options dialog box, which you open by clicking Options in the left pane of the Backstage view.

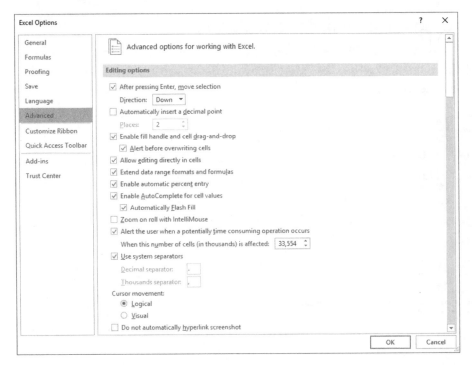

The Excel Options dialog box

The Excel Options dialog box has 10 separate pages of commands, organized by function. To display the General, Formulas, Proofing, Save, Language, Advanced, Customize Ribbon, Customize Quick Access Toolbar, Add-ins, or Trust Center page of the Excel Options dialog box, click the page name in the left pane.

Objective group 1
Create and manage worksheets and workbooks

The skills tested in this section of the Microsoft Office Specialist exam for Microsoft Excel 2016 relate to creating and managing workbooks and worksheets. Specifically, the following objectives are associated with this set of skills:

- **1.1** Create worksheets and workbooks   *CHAPTER 3 PART I*
- **1.2** Navigate in worksheets and workbooks
- **1.3** Format worksheets and workbooks
- **1.4** Customize options and views for worksheets and workbooks
- **1.5** Configure worksheets and workbooks for distribution

A single workbook can contain a vast amount of raw and calculated data stored on one or more worksheets. The data on a worksheet can be independent, or related to data in other areas of the workbook or in other workbooks.

You can structure and format workbook content so that key information can be easily identified and so that data is presented correctly on the screen and when printed. You can locate information within a workbook by searching values, formula elements, or named objects.

This chapter guides you in studying ways of creating, navigating in, displaying, formatting, saving, and printing workbooks and worksheets.

> To complete the practice tasks in this chapter, you need the practice files contained in the **MOSExcel2016\Objective1** practice file folder. For more information, see "Download the practice files" in this book's introduction.

Objective 1.1:
Create worksheets and workbooks

Create blank and prepopulated workbooks

When you start Excel 2016 without opening an existing workbook, a Start screen appears. From this screen you can open a recent workbook or create a new workbook —either a blank workbook based on the Normal template or a custom workbook based on another template. When Excel is running, you can create a blank or prepopulated workbook from the New page of the Backstage view.

The Start screen and New page display thumbnails of popular templates and templates that are specific to the season or an upcoming holiday. Some templates are installed on your computer with Office, and you can download others from the Office website.

Built-in and custom templates are available from the Featured and Custom views of the Start screen

If you create custom templates and save them in your Personal Templates folder, Featured and Custom or Personal links appear below the search box. You can click these links to switch between viewing program-supplied templates and your own. If you save templates in a location other than your Personal Templates folder, you can create workbooks based on those templates either from File Explorer or from the Open page of the Backstage view.

To create a new blank workbook

→ Start Excel. When the program **Start** screen appears, do either of the following:

- Press the **Esc** key.
- Click the **Blank workbook** thumbnail.

→ Display the **New** page of the Backstage view, and then click the **Blank workbook** thumbnail.

→ From the program window, press **Ctrl+N**.

To create a new workbook based on an installed template

→ From the **Start** screen or from the **New** page of the Backstage view, locate the template from which you want to create a workbook, and then do either of the following:

- Click the thumbnail to preview the template content, and then in the template information window, click **Create**.
- Double-click the thumbnail to create a workbook without previewing the template content.

To create a new workbook based on an online template

1. On the **Start** screen or on the **New** page of the Backstage view, do either of the following:

   - In the search box, enter a template type or subject and then press **Enter** or click the **Search button.**
   - Below the search box, click one of the suggested search topics to display templates of that type.

2. On the search results page, refine the results by clicking categories in the right pane.

3. Do either of the following:

    - Click the thumbnail to preview the template content, and then in the template information window, click **Create**.

    - Double-click the thumbnail to create a workbook without previewing the template content.

To create a new document based on a local template file

→ In File Explorer, navigate to the template location and then double-click the template.

Or

1. On the **Start** screen or on the **New** page of the Backstage view, click the **CUSTOM** or **PERSONAL** heading.

2. Locate the template you want to use, and then do either of the following:

    - Click the thumbnail to preview the template content, and then in the template information window, click **Create**.

    - Double-click the thumbnail to create a workbook without previewing the template content.

Add worksheets to workbooks

By default, a new workbook includes only one worksheet. You can add blank worksheets to the workbook or copy or move worksheets from another workbook.

 Tip When you create Excel objects such as charts, PivotTables, and PivotCharts, you can insert them on the worksheet that contains the data or on sheets that are dedicated to the new object.

To insert a new worksheet

→ Click the **New sheet** button at the right end of the worksheet tab section.

→ On the **Home** tab, in the **Cells** group, click the **Insert** arrow, and then click **Insert Sheet**.

Or

1. Right-click the worksheet tab before which you want to insert a new worksheet, and then click **Insert**.

2. On the **General** tab of the **Insert** dialog box, click **Worksheet**, and then click **OK**.

Move or copy worksheets

You can add worksheets to workbooks by moving or copying existing worksheets from other workbooks. You can also move worksheets within a workbook to reorder them.

To reorder worksheets within a workbook

→ On the tab bar, drag the tab of the worksheet you want to move to the new position.

To create a copy of a worksheet within a workbook

→ Press and hold **Ctrl** and then on the tab bar, drag the worksheet tab to the location where you want to create the copy.

To open the Move Or Copy dialog box

→ Right-click the worksheet tab, and then click **Move or Copy**.

→ On the **Home** tab, in the **Cells** group, click **Format**, and then in the **Organize Sheets** section, click **Move or Copy Sheet**.

To move a worksheet to another existing workbook

1. Open the source and destination workbooks in Excel.

   IMPORTANT You can move or copy a worksheet to an existing workbook only if that workbook is open.

2. In the source workbook, select the worksheet you want to move.

3. Open the **Move or Copy** dialog box, do the following, and then click **OK**:

   a. In the **To book** list, click the destination workbook.

   b. In the **Before sheet** box displaying the worksheets in the destination workbook, click the worksheet before which you want to insert the relocated worksheet.

To move a worksheet to its own workbook

1. Open the source workbook in Excel, and select the worksheet you want to move.

2. Open the **Move or Copy** dialog box.

3. In the **To book** list, click **(new book)**. Then click **OK**.

To create a copy of a worksheet in another existing workbook

1. Open the source and destination workbooks in Excel.

2. In the source workbook, select the worksheet you want to copy.

3. Open the **Move or Copy** dialog box, do the following, and then click **OK**:

   a. Select the **Create a copy** check box.

   b. In the **To book** list, click the destination workbook.

   c. In the **Before sheet** box displaying the worksheets in the destination workbook, click the worksheet before which you want to insert the relocated worksheet.

To copy a worksheet to its own workbook

1. Open the source workbook in Excel, and select the worksheet you want to copy.

2. Open the **Move or Copy** dialog box, do the following, and then click **OK**:

   a. Select the **Create a copy** check box.

   b. In the **To book** list, click **(new book)**.

Import data from delimited text files

If the content you want to use exists in another format, such as in a delimited text file, you can import the file contents into a worksheet in Excel.

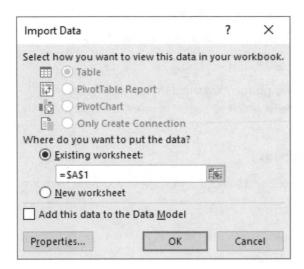

You can export delimited data from many other programs for reuse in Excel

Tip Importing a file disconnects the contents from the source file, whereas opening the file permits you to edit the file contents in Excel.

To import the contents of a text (.txt) or comma-separated values (.csv) file

1. On the **Data** tab, in the **Get External Data** group, click **From Text**.

2. In the **Import Text File** dialog box, browse to and select the text file you want to import, and then click **Import**.

3. On the **Step 1** page of the **Text Import Wizard**, click **Delimited** or **Fixed width** to indicate the way that data in the text file is separated. Specify the first row of data you want to import (this will almost always be 1), and select the **My data has headers** check box if applicable. Then click **Next**.

    Tip The preview at the bottom of the page displays the data being imported.

4. On the **Step 2** page of the **Text Import Wizard**, select the character or characters that separate the field content within the text file, and then click **Next**.

5. On the **Step 3** page of the **Text Import Wizard**, do the following, and then click **Finish**:

    • For each column of numeric data in the preview that requires specific number formatting, click the column and then specify the number format.

    • For each column you want to exclude from the import operation, click the column and then click **Do not import column (skip)**.

6. In the **Import Data** dialog box, click the location to which you want to import the data, and then click **OK**.

Objective 1.1 practice tasks

The practice file for these tasks is located in the **MOSExcel2016\Objective1** practice file folder. The folder also contains a subfolder of result files that you can use to check your work.

➤ Start Excel and then do the following:

  ❑ From the Start screen, create a new workbook based on the built-in *Blank workbook* template. Save the document in the practice file folder as <u>MyBlank.xlsx</u>.

  ❑ In the open workbook, display the New page of the Backstage view. Locate the online template for a <u>mortgage refinance calculator</u>. Create a workbook based on this template. Save the workbook in the practice file folder as <u>MyCalc.xls</u>.

➤ Open the **Excel_1-1** workbook and do the following:

  ❑ Move the **Source Data** worksheet so it is the last worksheet in the workbook.

  ❑ Add a copy of the **Source Data** worksheet to the open *MyBlank* workbook as the first worksheet in the workbook.

➤ Save the **Excel_1-1** and *MyBlank* workbooks.

➤ From the **Excel_1-1_Results** subfolder, open the **MyBlank_results**, **MyCalc_results**, and **Excel_1-1_results** files. Check your work by comparing the documents with those you created.

➤ Close the open workbooks.

Objective 1.2:
Navigate in worksheets and workbooks

Search for data within a workbook

You can easily locate specific values, formula content, comment text, and formatting anywhere within a workbook. Using the Find operation, you can search the entire workbook or a specific worksheet for text and formatting in formulas, calculated values, or comments.

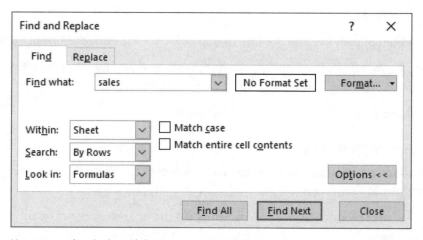

You can search a single worksheet or an entire workbook

To display the Find tab of the Find And Replace dialog box

→ On the **Home** tab, in the **Editing** group, display the **Find & Select** list, and then click **Find.**

→ Press **Ctrl+F.**

To search for text

1. Display the **Find** tab of the **Find and Replace** dialog box:

2. In the **Find what** box, enter the text you want to locate.

3. If the Options section is not expanded, click **Options** to display the search parameters, and then specify any of the following parameters:

- In the **Within** list, click **Sheet** or **Workbook**.
- In the **Search** list, click **By Rows** or **By Columns**.
- In the **Look in** list, click **Formulas**, **Values**, or **Comments**.
- Select the **Match case** or **Match entire cell contents** check boxes to further restrict your search.

4. Click **Find Next**.

To search for formatting

1. On the **Find** tab of the **Find and Replace** dialog box, click the **Format** button.
2. In the **Find Format** dialog box, specify the number, alignment, font, border, fill, or protection formatting you want to find. Then click **OK**.
3. In the **Find and Replace** dialog box, click **Find Next**.

To search for matching formatting

1. On the **Find** tab of the **Find and Replace** dialog box, click the **Format** arrow, and then click **Choose Format From Cell**.
2. When the pointer changes to an eyedropper, select the cell on which you want to base your search.
3. In the **Find and Replace** dialog box, click **Find Next**.

Navigate to a named cell, range, or workbook element

If you're looking for a specific element or type of element, you can locate it by using the Go To and Go To Special commands. From the Go To dialog box, you can locate any named element (such as a cell, cell range, named range, table, or chart). From the Go To Special dialog box, you can locate comments, formulas or specific formula elements, blank cells, objects, row or column differences, precedents and dependents, conditional formatting, data validation, and more.

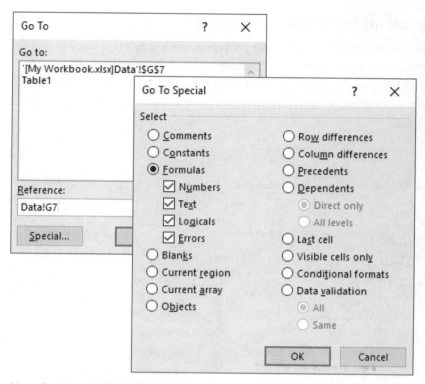

Move directly to specific workbook elements

To open the Go To Special dialog box

→ In the **Find & Select** list, click **Go To Special**.

→ Open the **Go To** dialog box, and then click the **Special** button.

To move to a named cell, range, or workbook element

→ On the formula bar, click the **Name** box arrow, and then select the named element.

→ Open the **Go To** dialog box. Click a named element in the **Go to** list, and then click **OK**.

To move to a location that has a specific property

1. Open the **Go To Special** dialog box.

2. In the **Select** area, click the property for which you want to search. Then click **OK**.

Link to internal and external locations and files

Excel worksheets can include hyperlinks that provide a quick way to connect to related information or to create a pre-addressed email message. You can create a hyperlink from any cell content to any of the hyperlink locations supported by the Office 2016 programs—another location on the worksheet, in the workbook, in an external document, or on the web.

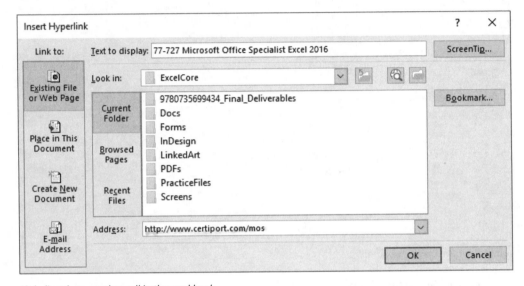

Link directly to another cell in the workbook

By default, hyperlinks are formatted as underlined, colored text. (The active and followed hyperlink colors are specified by the theme.) Clicking the hyperlink text in the cell that contains the hyperlink displays the hyperlink target.

Tip To select a cell that contains a hyperlink, click part of the cell away from the hyperlink or click and hold down the mouse button until the pointer changes to a plus sign.

To open the Insert Hyperlink dialog box

→ On the **Insert** tab, in the **Links** group, click the **Hyperlink** button.

→ Press **Ctrl+K**.

To create a hyperlink to a webpage

→ Enter a URL in the cell, and then press **Enter**.

Or

1. Select the cell or object you want to link from.

2. Open the **Insert Hyperlink** dialog box.

3. In the **Link to** list, click **Existing File or Web Page**. Then do either of the following:

   - In the **Address** box, enter the URL of the webpage you want to link to.

   - Click the **Browse the Web** button (the button labeled with a globe and magnifying glass). In the web browser window that opens (not a previously open window), display the webpage you want to link to. Move the window aside, if necessary, and click the **Insert Hyperlink** dialog box to copy the webpage address from the browser address bar to the **Address** box of the dialog box. Then minimize or close the browser window.

4. In the **Insert Hyperlink** dialog box, click **OK**.

Tip While inserting a hyperlink from a cell that contains text (not numeric data), the Text To Display box is active and displays the cell content. (Otherwise, it displays <<Selection in Document>>.) You can change the text in the cell by entering alternative text in the Text To Display box.

To link to an existing file or folder

1. Select the cell or object you want to link from.

2. Open the **Insert Hyperlink** dialog box, do the following, and then click **OK**:

   a. In the **Link to** list, click **Existing File or Web Page**.

   b. In the **Look in** area, browse to the file you want to link to, and double-click it to enter the file path and name in the Address box.

To create and link to an Excel workbook

1. Select the cell or object you want to link from, and then open the **Insert Hyperlink** dialog box.

2. In the **Link to** list, click **Create New Document**. Then review the location shown in the **Full path** section.

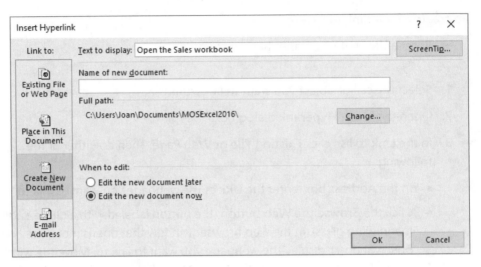

Simultaneously create a file and a link to it

3. If you want to create the new workbook in the folder shown in the **Full path** section, enter a name for the workbook in the **Name of new document** box. It is not necessary to append a file type extension.

Or, if you want to create the new workbook in a different folder, do the following:

a. Click the **Change** button.

b. In the **Create New Document** dialog box, browse to the folder in which you want to save the file.

c. In the **File Name** box, enter a name for the workbook, and append .xlsx to the workbook name to indicate the specific type of file you want to create. Then click **OK**.

4. In the **When to edit** area, do either of the following:

- To create a blank workbook, click **Edit the new document later**.
- To create a workbook and open it for editing, click **Edit the new document now**.

5. In the **Insert Hyperlink** dialog box, click **OK**.

6. If you chose the option to edit the workbook immediately, it opens now. Modify the file content as appropriate for the purposes of the hyperlink, and then save and close the file.

To create and link to a file of another type

1. Select the cell or object you want to link from, and then open the **Insert Hyperlink** dialog box.

2. In the **Link to** list, click **Create New Document**.

3. In the **Full path** section, click the **Change** button.

4. In the **Create New Document** dialog box, do the following, and then click **OK**:

   a. Browse to the folder in which you want to create the file.

   b. In the **Save as type** list, click the category of file you want to create.

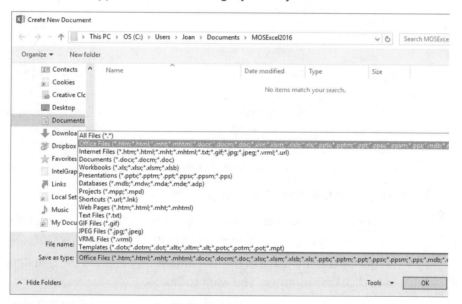

You can create and link to a wide variety of files

   c. In the **File Name** box, enter a name and file extension for the new file.

5. In the **When to edit** area, click **Edit the new document later** or **Edit the new document now**.

6. In the **Insert Hyperlink** dialog box, click **OK**.

7. If you chose the option to edit the file immediately, it opens now. Modify the file content as appropriate for the purposes of the hyperlink, and then save and close the file.

To link to a cell, worksheet, or named object in the workbook

1. Select the cell or object you want to link from, and then open the **Insert Hyperlink** dialog box.

2. In the **Link to** list, click **Place in This Document**.

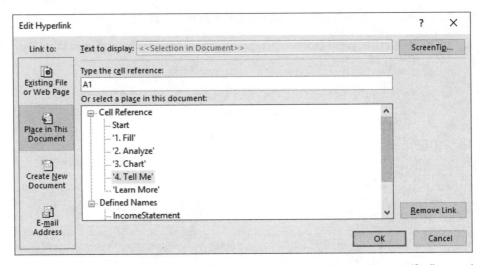

The Defined Names list includes objects such as tables and data ranges that you have specifically named

3. Do any of the following, and then click **OK**:

   - In the **Type the cell reference** box, enter a cell on the current worksheet or the path to a cell on another worksheet in the format *'WorksheetName'!A1*.

   - In the **Or select a place in this document** box, expand the **Cell Reference** list and click the worksheet you want to link to.

   - In the **Or select a place in this document** box, expand the **Defined Names** list and click the named object you want to link to.

To create a hyperlink that creates a pre-addressed email message

1. Select the cell or object you want to link from, and then open the **Insert Hyperlink** dialog box.

2. In the **Insert Hyperlink** dialog box, do the following, and then click **OK**:

   a. In the **Link to** list, click **E-mail Address**.

   b. Do either of the following:

      ○ In the **E-mail address** box, enter the email address of the message recipient.

      ○ In the **Recently used e-mail addresses** list, click an email address that you want to reuse.

   c. In the **Subject** box, enter the message subject.

To display alternative text when a user points to a hyperlink

1. In the **Insert Hyperlink** dialog box for the link, click the **ScreenTip** button.

2. In the **ScreenTip text** box, enter the text you want the ScreenTip to display.

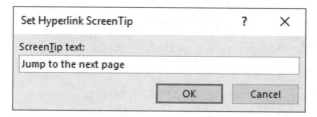

If you don't customize the ScreenTip, it displays the hyperlink destination and usage instructions

3. In the **ScreenTip text** box, click **OK**.

To edit a hyperlink

1. Right-click the hyperlink, and then click **Edit Hyperlink**.

2. In the **Edit Hyperlink** dialog box, modify any aspect of the hyperlink. Then click **OK**.

To remove a hyperlink

➜ Right-click the hyperlink, and then click **Remove Hyperlink**.

Objective 1.2 practice tasks

The practice file for these tasks is located in the **MOSExcel2016\Objective1** practice file folder. The folder also contains a result file that you can use to check your work.

➤ Open the **Excel_1-2** workbook and do the following:

❑ Search the workbook for all instances of the word garden. Confirm that the search returns results from both worksheets.

❑ Search the workbook for text that is formatted with a White font color. Change the font color to Orange to show that you found it.

➤ Display the **Product List** worksheet and do the following:

❑ Move to the first cell that contains a comment.

❑ Move to the cell range named *berry_bushes*.

❑ Move to cell F13.

❑ Create a hyperlink from cell F13 to the *berry_bushes* cell range.

❑ Move to the cell at the intersection of the last active row and column in the worksheet.

➤ Display the **Employees** worksheet and do the following:

❑ In cell C12, enter a hyperlink to the website located at www.adventure-works.com.

❑ Edit the hyperlink so that the cell displays Please visit our website instead of the URL.

➤ Save the **Excel_1-2** workbook.

➤ Open the **Excel_1-2_results** workbook. Compare the two workbooks to check your work.

➤ Close the open workbooks.

Objective 1.3:
Format worksheets and workbooks

Manage worksheet attributes

When creating new worksheets, Excel names them Sheet1, Sheet2, and so on. You can (and should) rename worksheets for these reasons:

- Workbook users can more easily locate and identify the context of information.
- You can reference worksheets in formulas by logical names.

You can assign colors to worksheet tabs, either to make them easily distinguishable or to categorize them.

To rename a worksheet

➜ Double-click the worksheet tab, enter the new worksheet name, and then press **Enter**.

Or

1. Do either of the following:

   - Right-click the worksheet tab, and then click **Rename**.

   - On the **Home** tab, in the **Cells** group, click **Format**, and then in the **Organize Sheets** section, click **Rename Sheet**.

2. Enter the new worksheet name, and then press **Enter**.

To change the color of a worksheet tab

➜ Right-click the tab, point to **Tab Color** in the shortcut menu, and then do either of the following:

   - Click a color in the **Theme Colors** or **Standard Colors** area.

   - Click **More Colors** to open the Colors dialog box, use the color controls to define a new color, and then click **OK**.

Manage rows and columns

An Excel 2016 worksheet can contain up to 1,048,576 rows and 16,384 columns of data. When you insert or delete rows and columns, you change the data structure on the worksheet rather than the worksheet itself. Inserting a row or column within a data range or table shifts existing content down or to the right; deleting a row or column shifts content up or to the left. Excel tidily updates any cell references within formulas to reflect the row and column changes.

Row height   Column width

	A	B	C	D	E	F	G
1							MO
2		Currently tracking ⬇			Original content	PM/CE1/Keystroke	AU Doc Review
3		Monday, October 10, 2016	Doc Pages	PDF Pages	Joan	Kathy	Joan
4		Working Days Budgeted ➡				2	1
5	a01	Title	1	1			
6	a02	LoC/copyright	1	1			
7	a03	Contents	4	4			
8	a04	Introduction	6	6	10-Sep		
9	a05	Taking a Microsoft Office Specialist Exam	4	4	10-Sep		
10	0	Exam 77-727 Microsoft Excel 2016	4	4	10-Sep		
11	1	Create and manage worksheets and workbooks	40	40	14-Sep	16-Sep	19-Sep
12	2	Manage data cells and ranges	30	30	14-Sep	16-Sep	19-Sep

Configure rows and columns to fit their contents

By default, Excel 2016 worksheet rows have a standard height of 12.75 points, or 0.17 inches, and their height increases and decreases to accommodate the number of lines in their longest entry, up to a maximum of 409 points. You can manually change the height of a row, but it is best to leave the row height dynamic to accommodate future changes, unless you have a good reason to specify a height. For example, you might want to specify a narrow row to create a visual break between blocks of data. (You can restore dynamic height adjustment if you need to.)

Worksheet columns have a standard width of 8.43 characters (in the default font), or 0.71 inches, and their width is not dynamic. You are more likely to want to change column width than row height, usually to accommodate long cell entries. You can have Excel adjust a column to fit its longest entry, or you can adjust it manually to up to 255 characters. In conjunction with text wrapping, adjusting column widths is a key technique for making as much data as possible visible on the screen or page.

Tip In Normal view, row heights are specified in points and column widths in characters. In Page Layout view, row heights and column widths are specified in inches (or your default unit of measure).

For the purposes of height and width adjustments, selecting a single cell in a row or column is the same as selecting the entire row or column. You can change the height or width of multiple rows or columns at the same time by selecting them and then performing the resizing operation.

See Also For information about inserting individual cells, see "Objective 2.1: Insert data in cells and ranges."

To insert rows or columns

1. Select the number of rows you want to insert, starting with the row above which you want the inserted rows to appear, or select the number of columns you want to insert, starting with the column to the left of which you want the inserted columns to appear.

2. Do either of the following:

    - On the **Home** tab, in the **Cells** group, click the **Insert** button.
    - Right-click the selection, and then click **Insert**.

To delete selected rows or columns

→ On the **Home** tab, in the **Cells** group, click the **Delete** button.

→ Right-click the selection, and then click **Delete**.

To change the height of one or more rows

→ Drag the bottom border of the row selector up or down.

Tip As you drag the border, a ScreenTip displays the current row height in either points or inches and in pixels.

Or

1. Select the row or rows you want to change.

2. Do either of the following:

    - Right-click the selection, and then click **Row Height**.

    - On the **Home** tab, in the **Cells** group, display the **Format** list, and then click **Row Height**.

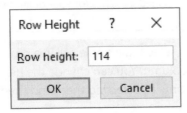

Set a specific row height of up to 409 points

3. In the **Row Height** dialog box, specify the height you want, and then click **OK**.

To change the width of a column

→ Drag the right border of the column selector to the left or right.

> **Tip** As you drag the border, a ScreenTip displays the current column width in either characters or inches and in pixels.

Or

1. Select the column or columns whose width you want to change.

2. Do either of the following:

    - Right-click the selection, and then click **Column Width**.

    - On the **Home** tab, in the **Cells** group, display the **Format** list, and then click **Column Width**.

3. In the **Column Width** dialog box, specify the width you want, and then click **OK**.

To size a column or row to fit its contents

→ Double-click the right border of the column heading or the bottom border of the row heading.

→ Select the column. On the **Home** tab, in the **Cells** group, display the **Format** list, and then click **AutoFit Column Width**.

→ Select the row. On the **Home** tab, in the **Cells** group, display the **Format** list, and then click **AutoFit Row Height**.

Tip You can adjust the width of all the columns in a worksheet at the same time. Click the worksheet selector to select the entire worksheet, and then double-click the border between any two columns. Every populated column resizes to fit its contents. Empty columns remain unchanged.

Change the appearance of workbook content

You can enhance the look of an entire workbook by applying a predefined theme—a combination of colors, fonts, and effects. In the Themes gallery, you can point to a theme to display a live preview of its effect on the workbook elements before you apply it.

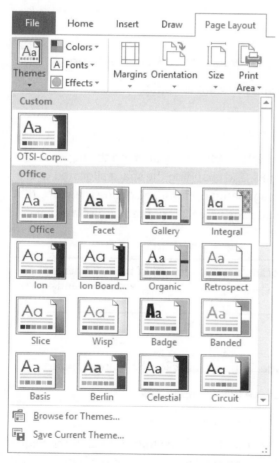

The Office section of the gallery displays thumbnails of built-in themes

The theme applied to the workbook controls the font and fill colors of existing text and objects, and of content that you add to the workbook later. You can apply only one theme to a workbook; individual worksheets can't have different themes.

If you like certain aspects of different themes (for example, the colors of one theme and the fonts of another), you can mix and match theme elements. If you create a combination of theme elements that you would like to use with other workbooks, you can save the combination as a custom theme.

> **Exam Strategy** Exam 77-727 requires you to demonstrate the ability to apply a built-in theme to a workbook. Modifying themes and creating custom themes is part of the objective domain for Exam 77-728: Microsoft Excel 2016 Expert.

To apply a theme to a workbook

1. On the **Page Layout** tab, in the **Themes** group, click the **Themes** button.

2. In the **Themes** gallery, click the theme you want to apply.

Modify page setup

You can control the basic footprint of printed worksheets by defining the paper size and orientation, changing the page margins, and changing the space allocated to the header and footer. By configuring these page setup options, you define the space that is available for the content on an individual page when it is printed or displayed in Print Layout view.

> **Tip** If your content doesn't fit within the allocated area, you can adjust the way it fits on the page by scaling it. For more information, see "Objective 1.5: Configure worksheets and workbooks for distribution."

To change the page margins

1. On the **Page Layout** tab, in the **Page Setup** group, click the **Margins** button.

2. On the **Margins** menu, do either of the following:

   - Click the standard margin setting you want.

   - Click the **Custom Margins** command. Then on the **Margins** tab of the **Page Setup** dialog box, specify the **Top**, **Bottom**, **Left**, and **Right** margins, and click **OK**.

1

To change the page orientation

→ On the **Page Layout** tab, in the **Page Setup** group, click the **Orientation** button, and then click **Portrait** or **Landscape**.

To set a standard paper size

→ On the **Page Layout** tab, in the **Page Setup** group, click the **Size** button, and then click the paper size you want.

To set a custom paper size

1. On the **Page Layout** tab, in the **Page Setup** group, click the **Size** button, and then click **More Paper Sizes**.

2. On the **Page** tab of the **Page Setup** dialog box, click **Options**.

3. On the **Paper/Quality** tab of the **Printer Properties** dialog box, in the **Paper Options** area, click **Custom**.

4. In the **Custom Paper Size** dialog box, enter a name for the custom size, enter the width and length of the paper, specify the units of measurement, click **Save**, and then click **Close**.

5. Click **OK** in each of the open dialog boxes.

Tip The available print settings depend on the currently selected printer.

Insert headers and footers

You can display information on every page of a printed worksheet, and also in Page Layout view, by inserting it in the page headers and footers. You can have a different header and footer on the first page or different headers and footers on odd and even pages. When you create a header or footer, Excel displays the workbook in a view that is similar to Page Layout view, and the Design tool tab appears on the ribbon.

An active header or footer is divided into three sections. You can insert content directly into the worksheet header sections, or build the content in the Header dialog box.

You can enter document information and properties such as the current or total page number, current date or time, file path, file name, or sheet name from the Design tool tab, or you can enter and format text the same way you would in the worksheet body. You can also insert an image, such as a company logo.

To insert a standard header or footer

1. On the **Page Layout** tab, in the **Page Setup** group, click the dialog box launcher.

2. In the **Page Setup** dialog box, click the **Header/Footer** tab.

3. In the **Header** list or **Footer** list, click the content you want to display in that area.

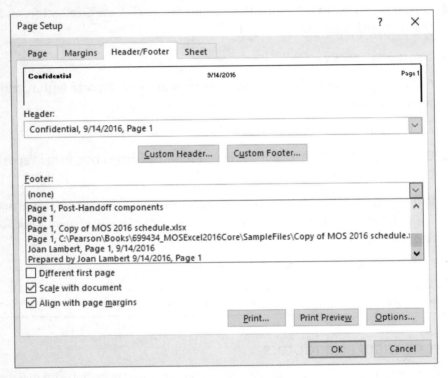

Select from standard document properties or create a custom entry

4. In the **Page Setup** dialog box, click **OK**.

Tip You can't format header or footer text from within the Page Setup dialog box, but you can insert the content and then format it in Page Layout view.

To build a custom header

1. On the **Header/Footer** tab of the **Page Setup** dialog box, click the **Custom Header** or **Custom Footer** button.

2. Click the left, center, or right box to edit the corresponding section of the header or footer.

3. Do any of the following:

- Insert text, then select the text and click the **Format Text** button to change the font formatting.

- Click the buttons to insert document properties such as page number, number of pages, date, time, file path, file name, and worksheet name.

- Click the **Insert Picture** button to insert a local or online image.

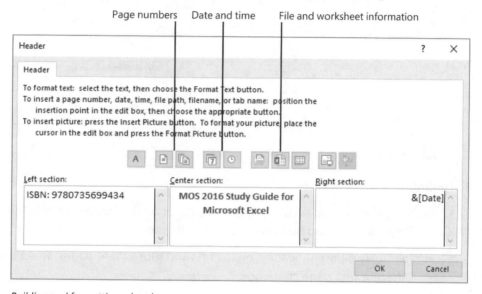

Building and formatting a header

4. When you finish, click **OK** in the **Header** or **Footer** dialog box, and in the **Page Setup** dialog box.

To activate the page header area of the worksheet

→ In **Normal** view, on the **Insert** tab, in the **Text** group, click **Header & Footer**.

→ In **Page Layout** view, at the top of the page, click **Add header**.

To activate the page footer area of the worksheet

→ In **Normal** view, on the **Insert** tab, in the **Text** group, click **Header & Footer**. Then on the **Design** tool tab, click **Go to Footer**.

→ In **Page Layout** view, at the bottom of the page, click **Add footer**.

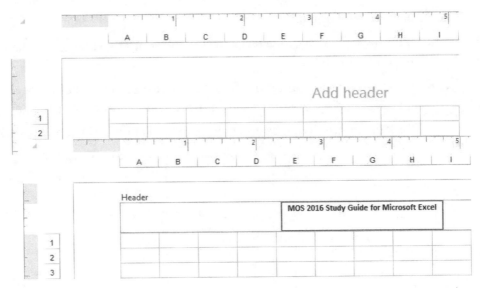

Adding a header in Page Layout view

To configure header options

1. In the **Options** group on the **Design** tool tab, or on the **Header/Footer** tab of the **Page Setup** dialog box, do either of the following:

    -   To display different headers on the first and subsequent pages, select the **Different first page** check box.

    -   To display different headers on odd and even pages, select the **Different odd and even pages** check box.

2. Review the page headers and footers and ensure that the correct information appears on the first, subsequent, odd, and even pages.

To close the header or footer area

➜ Click anywhere in the worksheet body.

Tip If you decide to insert a header or footer just before printing, you can do so from the Header/Footer tab of the Page Setup dialog box, which is accessible from the Print page of the Backstage view.

To edit the header or footer

➜ Activate the header or footer, and then make your changes.

Objective 1.3 practice tasks

The practice file for these tasks is located in the **MOSExcel2016\Objective1** practice file folder. The folder also contains a result file that you can use to check your work.

➤ Open the **Excel_1-3** workbook and do the following:

❑ Change each of the worksheet tabs to a different color from the theme color palette.

❑ Apply the *Retrospect* theme to the workbook. Verify that the worksheet tab colors change.

❑ Change the worksheet names from **JanFeb**, **MarApr**, **MayJun**, **JulAug**, **SepOct**, and **NovDec** to <u>Period1</u>, <u>Period2</u>, <u>Period3</u>, <u>Period4</u>, <u>Period5</u>, and <u>Period6</u>.

➤ Display the *Period1* worksheet and do the following:

❑ Delete column A (Day) and row 2 (Hour).

❑ Configure the worksheet to print at a Landscape orientation. Display the print preview of the worksheet to verify the settings.

❑ Create a header that will print on all the pages of the worksheet. In the left header section, enter the Current Date property; in the center section, enter the File Name property; and in the right section, enter the Page Number property.

❑ Change the center section of the header to display the name of the worksheet instead of the workbook.

➤ Display the *Period2* worksheet and do the following:

❑ Resize columns D:O to fit their content.

❑ Check the width of column D, and then set column C to the same width.

➤ Save the **Excel_1-3** workbook.

➤ Open the **Excel_1-3_results** workbook. Compare the two workbooks to check your work. Then close the open workbooks.

Objective 1.4: Customize options and views for worksheets and workbooks

Hide or unhide content

A workbook, particularly one that contains data calculations, PivotTables, or PivotCharts, might contain reference data that isn't otherwise required. You can hide rows, columns, or entire worksheets of data you don't need to use or don't want other people to see.

When you hide rows or columns, anyone who notices that column letters or row numbers are missing can unhide the information unless you protect the workbook. If you don't want to go to the trouble of enforcing protection, you can hide the row and column headings so that the hidden information is not as obvious. This leaves only a small gap in place of any hidden rows or columns. To entirely mask the rows and columns, you can also hide the gridlines.

Hide columns, rows, or entire worksheets

To hide selected rows or columns

➜ Right-click the selection, and then click **Hide**.

Or

1. On the **Home** tab, in the **Cells** group, display the **Format** list.

2. In the **Visibility** section of the **Format** list, point to **Hide & Unhide**, and then click **Hide Rows** to hide the selected row(s) or **Hide Columns** to hide the selected column(s).

To find hidden rows or columns in a worksheet

➜ Open the **Go To Special** dialog box, click **Visible cells only**, and then click **OK**. In the highlighted content, cells adjacent to hidden cells have a thin white border.

To unhide rows or columns

1. Select the columns or rows on both sides of the hidden column(s) or row(s).

2. Right-click the selection, and then click **Unhide**.

Or

1. Select the rows or columns on both sides of the hidden rows or columns.

2. On the **Home** tab, in the **Cells** group, display the **Format** list.

3. In the **Visibility** section of the **Format** list, point to **Hide & Unhide**, and then click **Unhide Rows** to display the hidden row(s) or **Unhide Columns** to display the hidden column(s).

To unhide the first row or column of a worksheet

1. In the **Name** box to the left of the formula bar, enter <u>A1</u>, and then press **Enter**.

2. On the **Home** tab, in the **Cells** group, display the **Format** list.

3. In the **Visibility** section of the **Format** list, point to **Hide & Unhide**, and then click **Unhide Rows** to display row 1, or **Unhide Columns** to display column A.

To hide a worksheet

➜ Right-click the worksheet tab, and then click **Hide**.

To display a hidden worksheet

1. Right-click any visible worksheet tab, and then click **Unhide**.

2. In the **Unhide** dialog box, select the worksheet you want to display, and then click **OK**.

Customize the Quick Access Toolbar

By default, buttons representing the Save, Undo, and Redo commands (and the Touch/Mouse Mode command, when you're working on a touchscreen device) appear on the Quick Access Toolbar in the Excel program window. If you regularly use a few commands that are scattered on various tabs of the ribbon and you don't want to switch between tabs to access the commands, you can add them to the Quick Access Toolbar so that they're always available to you. You can add commands to the Quick Access Toolbar from the Customize Quick Access Toolbar menu (which includes eight additional common commands), from the ribbon, or from the Excel Options dialog box. You can add any type of command to the Quick Access Toolbar, even a drop-down list of options or gallery of thumbnails.

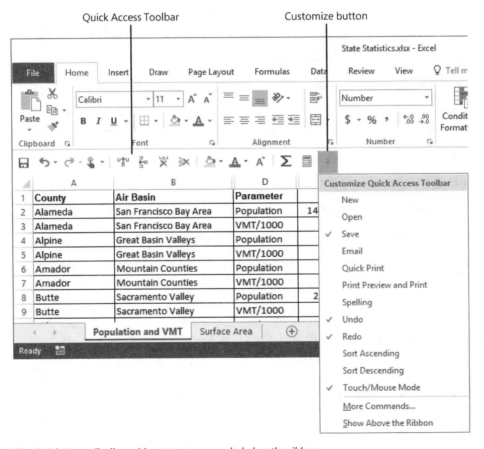

The Quick Access Toolbar with custom commands, below the ribbon

You save time by placing frequently used commands on the Quick Access Toolbar. To save even more time, you can move the Quick Access Toolbar from its default position above the ribbon to below the ribbon, so your mouse has less distance to travel from the content you're working with to the command you want to invoke. If you add all the buttons you use most often to the Quick Access Toolbar, you can hide the ribbon to gain screen space.

You can modify the Quick Access Toolbar by adding, moving, separating, or removing commands. You can add commands in several ways, but you can modify and separate commands only from the Excel Options dialog box. From that dialog box, you can modify the Quick Access Toolbar that appears in the program window or create a custom Quick Access Toolbar that appears only in the currently active workbook.

To display the Quick Access Toolbar page of the Excel Options dialog box

➜ Right-click a blank area of the ribbon, and then click **Customize Quick Access Toolbar**.

➜ Click the **Customize Quick Access Toolbar** button, and then click **More Commands**.

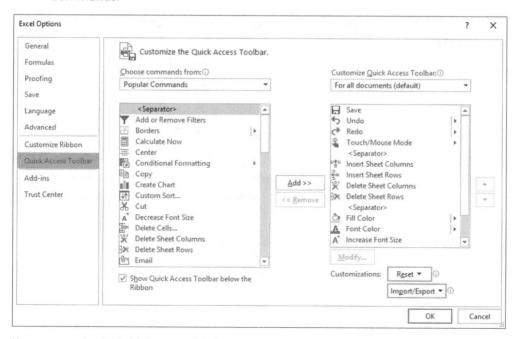

You can customize the Quick Access Toolbar for all workbooks or create one unique to the current workbook

To add commands to the Quick Access Toolbar

→ Click the **Customize Quick Access Toolbar** button, and then click one of the common commands displayed on the menu.

→ Right-click a command on the ribbon, and then click **Add to Quick Access Toolbar**.

Or

1. Display the **Quick Access Toolbar** page of the **Excel Options** dialog box.

2. In the **Choose commands from** list, click the group of commands from which you want to select.

3. In the **Choose commands** pane, locate the command you want to add, and then click the **Add** button.

4. In the **Excel Options** dialog box, click **OK**.

To remove a command from the Quick Access Toolbar

→ Right-click the command on the **Quick Access Toolbar**, and then click **Remove from Quick Access Toolbar**.

→ On the **Customize Quick Access Toolbar** menu, click any active command (indicated by a check mark) to remove it.

→ On the **Quick Access Toolbar** page of the **Excel Options** dialog box, in the **Customize Quick Access Toolbar** pane, click the command. Then click the **Remove** button.

To change the order of commands on the Quick Access Toolbar

→ On the **Quick Access Toolbar** page of the **Excel Options** dialog box, in the **Customize Quick Access Toolbar** pane, click the command you want to move. Then click **Move Up** to move the command to the left or **Move Down** to move it to the right.

To separate commands on the Quick Access Toolbar

→ On the **Quick Access Toolbar** page of the **Excel Options** dialog box, in the **Customize Quick Access Toolbar** pane, click the command after which you want to insert a separator. At the top of the **Choose commands** pane, click **<Separator>**. Then click **Add**.

To create a Quick Access Toolbar that is specific to the current workbook

→ On the **Quick Access Toolbar** page of the **Excel Options** dialog box, in the **Customize Quick Access Toolbar** list, click **For** *document name*. Then add buttons to the toolbar as usual.

To change the location of the Quick Access Toolbar

→ On the **Customize Quick Access Toolbar** menu, click **Show Below the Ribbon** or **Show Above the Ribbon**.

→ Right-click the **Quick Access Toolbar**, and then click **Show Quick Access Toolbar Below the Ribbon** or **Show Quick Access Toolbar Above the Ribbon**.

→ On the **Quick Access Toolbar** page of the **Excel Options** dialog box, select or clear the **Show Quick Access Toolbar below the Ribbon** check box.

To reset the Quick Access Toolbar to its default content

→ On the **Quick Access Toolbar** page of the **Excel Options** dialog box, click the **Reset** button, and then click **Reset only Quick Access Toolbar** or **Reset all customizations**.

Tip Resetting the Quick Access Toolbar doesn't change its location.

Modify the display of worksheets

Switch among views

From the View toolbar at the bottom of the program window, or from the View tab, you can switch among three views of a worksheet:

- **Normal** The worksheet is displayed in the window at 100 percent magnification or the zoom level you select. Page breaks are indicated by black dashed lines.

- **Page Layout** Each worksheet page is displayed on screen as it will be printed, with space between the individual pages. If the display of rulers is on, rulers appear on the top and left edges of the window. The page header and footer are visible and you can select them for editing.

- **Page Break Preview** The entire worksheet is displayed in the window, with page breaks indicated by bold blue dashed lines and page numbers displayed in the center of each page. You can change the page breaks by dragging the blue lines.

Buttons for changing the view are located on the View tab of the ribbon and on the View Shortcuts toolbar near the right end of the status bar.

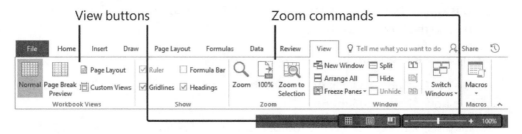

View and Zoom commands on the toolbar and status bar

To display a standard worksheet view

→ On the **View** tab, in the **Workbook Views** group, click the **Normal**, **Page Layout**, or **Page Break Preview** button.

→ On the **View Shortcuts** toolbar near the right end of the status bar, click the **Normal**, **Page Layout**, or **Page Break Preview** button.

Magnify the worksheet

From the Zoom toolbar at the bottom of the program window, or from the Zoom group on the View tab, you can change the zoom level of a worksheet in any range from 10 percent to 400 percent. You can zoom the entire worksheet or select a range of cells and have Excel determine the zoom level necessary to fit the selection in the window.

To zoom in or out in 10-percent increments

→ On the status bar, click the **Zoom In** (+) or **Zoom Out** (-) button.

To change the zoom level dynamically

→ Drag the **Zoom** slider to the left to zoom out or to the right to zoom in.

To zoom to a specific magnification

1. Do either of the following:

   • On the **View** tab, in the **Zoom** group, click the **Zoom** button.

   • On the status bar, click the **Zoom level** button.

2. In the **Zoom** dialog box, click a specific magnification level, or click **Custom** and then enter a value from 10 to 400. Then click **OK**.

To zoom in on selected cells

1. Select the cell or cell range you want to zoom in on.

2. Do either of the following:

   - On the **View** tab, in the **Zoom** group, click the **Zoom to Selection** button.

   - Open the **Zoom** dialog box, click **Fit selection**, and then click **OK**.

Display formulas

Many worksheets contain formulas for the purpose of calculating data. A formula is visible in the formula bar when you click the cell that contains it, but its resulting value is visible in the cell. If you need to review multiple formulas, it is easier to do so if you first display them.

To display formulas in a worksheet

→ On the **Formulas** tab, in the **Formula Auditing** group, click the **Show Formulas** button.

→ Press **Ctrl+`**.

Display multiple parts of a workbook in one window

It can be cumbersome to work in a worksheet that is too long or wide to display legibly in the program window, to scroll up and down or back and forth to view data elsewhere in the worksheet, or to switch back and forth between multiple worksheets in the same workbook if you frequently need to access information in both of them.

You can view multiple parts of a worksheet at one time by freezing rows or columns so they stay in view while you scroll the rest of the worksheet, by splitting the window so you can independently scroll and work in two or four views of the worksheet within the same program window, or by displaying multiple instances of the workbook in separate program windows. Regardless of the technique you use, changes you make to the workbook content in any one view are immediately reflected in the others.

Tip Another way to display disparate rows or columns together on one screen is to hide the rows or columns between them.

To freeze the first row or column of a worksheet

→ On the **View** tab, in the **Window** group, click the **Freeze Panes** button, and then click **Freeze Top Row** or **Freeze First Column**.

To freeze multiple rows or columns

1. Select the row below or column to the right of those you want to freeze, by clicking the row selector or column selector.

2. On the **View** tab, in the **Window** group, click the **Freeze Panes** button, and then click **Freeze Panes**.

To simultaneously freeze columns and rows

1. Select the cell that is below and to the right of the intersection of the row and column you want to freeze.

2. On the **View** tab, in the **Window** group, click the **Freeze Panes** button, and then click **Freeze Panes**.

Tip You can freeze as many columns and rows as you like depending on what cell is selected when you invoke the Freeze Panes command. Selecting a cell in row 1 freezes the columns to the left of that cell. Selecting a cell in column A freezes the rows above that cell. Selecting cell A1 freezes the panes at the midpoint of the current window (the top half of the rows and the left half of the columns). Selecting a cell other than those in row 1 and column A freezes the rows above and columns to the left of the cell.

To unfreeze all rows and columns

→ On the **View** tab, in the **Window** group, click the **Freeze Panes** button, and then click **Unfreeze Panes**.

To split a workbook

1. Do either of the following:

   • To split the window into two parts, click a cell in row 1 or column A.

   • To split the window into four parts, click the cell that you want to designate as the inside corner of the lower-right quadrant.

2. On the **View** tab, in the **Window** group, click **Split**.

To modify the split between windows

→ Drag the vertical or horizontal split bar to the row or column where you want to split the window.

To remove a split from a program window

→ Double-click a split bar to remove it.

→ Drag a vertical split bar to the top of the scroll bar to remove it.

→ Drag a horizontal split bar to the right end of the scroll bar to remove it.

→ On the **View** toolbar, click the active **Split** button to remove all splits.

To display multiple views of a workbook in separate program windows

1. On the **View** tab, in the **Window** group, click the **New Window** button to open another instance of the workbook.

   Tip You can open several instances of the workbook; Excel displays the instance number after the workbook name in the program window title bar.

2. Arrange the workbook windows as you want, or click the **Arrange All** button and then in the **Arrange Windows** dialog box, click **Tiled**, **Horizontal**, **Vertical**, or **Cascade**. To arrange only the instances of the active workbook, select the **Windows of active workbook** check box. Then click **OK**.

3. Display the worksheet, worksheet section, or workbook element you want in each workbook window.

4. To return to a single program window, close the others. It is not necessary to save changes in any but the last open instance of the workbook.

Modify document properties

Before distributing a workbook, you might want to attach properties to it so that the file is readily identifiable in the Details view of any browsing dialog box, such as the Open dialog box. In Excel 2016, workbook properties are easily accessible from the Info page of the Backstage view. You can view and modify some properties directly on the Info page, or you can work in the Properties dialog box.

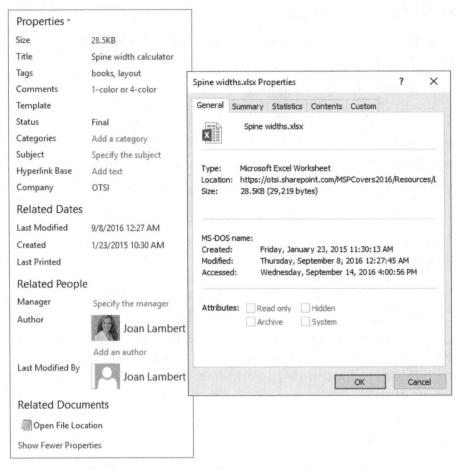

Workbook properties can be used to locate a workbook in File Explorer or on a SharePoint site

To set or change a basic property

→ On the **Info** page of the Backstage view, click the property to activate it, and then add or change information.

To display additional common properties

→ On the **Info** page of the Backstage view, click **Show All Properties**.

To display all properties in the Properties dialog box

→ On the **Info** page of the Backstage view, click **Properties**, and then click **Advanced Properties**.

→ In File Explorer, right-click the file, and then click **Properties**.

Objective 1.4 practice tasks

The practice file for these tasks is located in the **MOSExcel2016\Objective1** practice file folder. The folder also contains a result file that you can use to check your work.

➤ Open the **Excel_1-4** workbook, display the **Inventory List** worksheet, and do the following:

❏ Hide column A (the Inventory ID) and row 3 (the data sources).

❏ Add the Calculator button (which is not available on any ribbon tab) to the Quick Access Toolbar. Make it the leftmost button, and insert a separator between it and the other buttons.

❏ Create a Quick Access Toolbar for only the current workbook. Add the Insert Combo Chart, Insert Picture, and Insert Table buttons (all available on the Insert tab). Then display the Quick Access Toolbar below the ribbon.

❏ Hide the **By Product-Customer Filtered** worksheet.

➤ Display the **My Monthly Budget** worksheet and do the following:

❏ Freeze rows 1 through 9 so that when you scroll the rest of the worksheet, those rows are always visible.

❏ Split the worksheet so that you can display rows 1 through 9 in the top window and scroll the budget data in the bottom window.

❏ Attach the keywords (tags) *spending* and *saving* to the workbook.

❏ Display the **My Monthly Budget** worksheet in Page Layout view.

❏ Select the *Projected Monthly Income* section of the worksheet, and zoom in to display only the selected cells.

➤ Save the **Excel_1-4** workbook and open the **Excel_1-4_results** workbook. Compare the two workbooks to check your work. Then close the open workbooks.

Objective 1.5: Configure worksheets and workbooks for distribution

Print all or part of a workbook

An Excel workbook can contain many separate worksheets of data. You can print part or all of an individual worksheet, a selected worksheet, or all the worksheets that contain content at one time.

Select the printing scope

By default, Excel prints only the currently active worksheet or worksheet group. You can choose specific print scopes from the Print page of the Backstage view.

To print all populated worksheets in a workbook

→ On the **Print** page of the Backstage view, in the first list in the **Settings** area, click **Print Entire Workbook**.

To print a single worksheet

1. Display the worksheet you want to print.

2. On the **Print** page of the Backstage view, in the **Settings** area, click **Print Active Sheets** in the first list.

To print specific worksheets

1. Group the worksheets that you want to print.

2. On the **Print** page of the Backstage view, in the **Settings** area, click **Print Active Sheets** in the first list.

To print a portion of a worksheet

1. On the worksheet, select the range of cells you want to print.

2. On the **Print** page of the Backstage view, in the **Settings** area, click **Print Selection** in the first list.

Define a print area

If you want to print only part of a worksheet, you can do so from the Print page of the Backstage view as described earlier in this chapter. Alternatively, if you will often print the same portion of a worksheet, you can define that portion as the print area.

After defining the print area of a workbook, you can add selected ranges to it. A range that is contiguous to the original range becomes part of the original print area definition; a range that is noncontiguous or a different shape becomes a separate print area and is printed on a separate page. You can also remove ranges from the print area.

If you don't want to limit printing to the print area, you can permanently clear the print area or you can temporarily ignore it when printing the worksheet.

To define a selected range as the print area

➜ On the **Page Layout** tab, in the **Page Setup** group, click the **Print Area** button, and then click **Set Print Area**.

To add a selected range to a defined print area

➜ On the **Page Layout** tab, in the **Page Setup** group, click the **Print Area** button, and then click **Add to Print Area**.

> **Tip** The Add To Print Area option is not displayed when the selected area of the worksheet is already part of the designated print area.

To remove a range from the print area

1. On the **Page Layout** tab, click the **Page Setup** dialog box launcher.

2. On the **Sheet** tab of the **Page Setup** dialog box, change the range reference in the **Print area** box, and then click **OK**.

To clear the print area

➜ On the **Page Layout** tab, in the **Page Setup** group, click the **Print Area** button, and then click **Clear Print Area**.

To ignore the print area

➜ On the **Print** page of the Backstage view, in the **Settings** area, click **Ignore Print Area** in the first list.

> **Tip** The Ignore Print Area setting remains active (indicated by a check mark) until you turn it off by clicking it again.

Save workbooks in alternative file formats

You can save a workbook in multiple locations and in multiple formats.

Where once it was common only to save a file locally on your computer, many people now save files to shared locations such as Microsoft SharePoint sites, OneDrive folders, and OneDrive for Business folders for the purpose of collaborating with other people or accessing the files from multiple computers and devices.

The 2007 Microsoft Office system introduced a new set of file formats based on XML, called Microsoft Office Open XML Formats. By default, Excel 2016 workbooks are saved in the .xlsx format, which is an Excel-specific Open XML format. The .xlsx format provides the following benefits:

- File sizes are smaller than with previous file formats.

- It is simpler to recover damaged content because XML files can be opened in a variety of text editors.

- Security is greater because .xlsx files cannot contain macros, and personal data can easily be identified and removed from files.

Workbooks saved in the .xlsx format can be opened by Excel 2016, Excel 2013, Excel 2010, and Excel 2007. Users of earlier versions of Excel can download a converter that they can use to open an .xlsx file in their version of Excel.

In addition to saving a workbook for use with Excel 2016, you can save it in other formats, including the following:

- **Excel Macro-Enabled Workbook** To be able to store VBA macro code, use the XML-based .xlsm format.

- **Excel 97-2003** If you intend to share an Excel workbook specifically with users of Excel 2003 or earlier, you can save it in the .xls file format used by those versions of the program. Downgrading the file removes any unsupported formatting and features.

- **Single File Web Page or Web Page** You can convert a workbook into HTML so that it can be viewed in a web browser. Saving a workbook in the Single File Web Page format creates one .mht or .mhtml file that contains the content and supporting information, whereas saving a workbook in the Web Page format creates one .htm or .html file that sets up the display structure and a folder that contains separate content and supporting information files.

- **Excel Template** To be able to use a workbook as the starting point for other workbooks, you can save the file as a template.

- **Delimited text file** To share data from an Excel workbook with other programs, you can save it as a text file that contains tab-delimited or comma-delimited content. Saving a workbook in a text file format removes formatting and unsupported objects.

If you want people to be able to view a workbook exactly as it appears on your screen, use one of these two formats:

- **PDF (.pdf)** This format is preferred by commercial printing facilities. Recipients can display the file in the free Microsoft Reader or Adobe Reader programs, and can display and edit the file in Word 2016 or Adobe Acrobat.

- **XPS (.xps)** This format precisely renders all fonts, images, and colors. Recipients can display the file in the free Microsoft Reader program or the free XPS Viewer program.

The PDF and XPS formats are designed to deliver workbooks as electronic representations of the way they appear when printed. Both types of files can easily be sent by email to many recipients and can be made available on a webpage for downloading by anyone who wants them. However, the files are no longer Excel workbooks and cannot be opened or edited in Excel.

When you save an Excel workbook in PDF or XPS format, you can optimize the file size of the document for your intended distribution method—the larger Standard file size is better for printing, whereas the Minimum file size is suitable for online publishing. You can also configure the following options:

- Specify the pages and worksheets to include in the PDF or XPS file.

- Include or exclude non-printing elements such as properties.

- Create an ISO-compliant PDF file.

IMPORTANT If you have Adobe Acrobat installed on your computer, that program might install additional tools that you can use to create PDF files from within Office programs. For example, you might have a custom Acrobat tab on the ribbon, a Save As Adobe PDF command in the left pane of the Backstage view, or a Create Adobe PDF button in the Export page of the Backstage view. When demonstrating the ability to perform tasks during the Microsoft Office Specialist exam, you can use only the built-in Excel functionality, which this book describes.

To open the Save As dialog box

➜ On the **Save As** page of the Backstage view, do any of the following:

- Below the Places list, click the **Browse** button.
- Above the file navigation controls, click the file path.
- Below the file navigation controls, click the **More options** link.

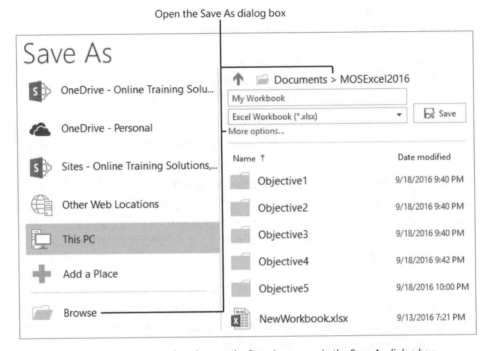

You can navigate through storage locations on the Save As page or in the Save As dialog box

➜ On the **Export** page of the Backstage view, click **Change File Type**, click the file type you want, and then click **Save As**.

To save a file in an alternative file format with the default settings

➜ On the **Save As** page of the Backstage view, in the file type list at the top of the right column, click the format you want. Then click the **Save** button.

➜ In the **Save As** dialog box, in the **Save as type** list, click the format you want, and then click **Save**.

➜ On the **Export** page of the Backstage view, click **Change File Type**, click the file type you want, and click **Save As**. Then in the **Save As** dialog box that opens, click **Save**.

1

To save a file in PDF or XPS format with custom settings

1. On the **Export** page of the Backstage view, click **Create PDF/XPS Document**, and then click the **Create PDF/XPS** button.

2. In the **Publish as PDF or XPS** dialog box, click **Options**.

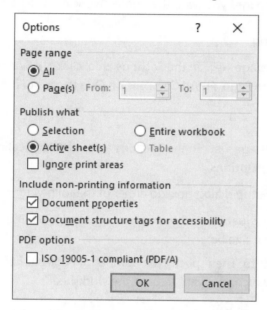

You can choose to include only specific worksheets or worksheet areas when saving a workbook as a PDF file

3. In the **Options** dialog box, select the options you want for the PDF or XPS file, and then click **OK**.

Or

1. Open the **Save As** dialog box. In the **Save as type** list, click either **PDF** or **XPS Document**.

2. In the **Save As** dialog box, click **Options**.

3. In the **Options** dialog box, select the options you want for the PDF or XPS file, and then click **OK**.

> **Exam Strategy** Ensure that you are familiar with the types of file formats in which you can save Excel workbooks and when it is appropriate to use each one.

Set print scaling

If your worksheet content doesn't fit naturally within the space allocated to it on the page, you can scale the content for the purpose of printing, instead of modifying the content to make it fit. You can scale the worksheet manually or allow Excel to scale it for you by specifying the number of pages you want the printed worksheet to be.

To scale the worksheet when printing

→ On the **Print** page of the Backstage view, in the **Settings** area, click **No Scaling**, and then click **Fit Sheet on One Page**, **Fit All Columns on One Page**, or **Fit All Rows on One Page**.

Or

1. On the **Print** page of the Backstage view, in the **Settings** area, click **No Scaling**, and then click **Custom Scaling Options**.

2. On the **Page** tab of the **Page Setup** dialog box, do either of the following:

   - In the **Scaling** area, click **Adjust to**, and then enter or select a scaling percentage in the **% normal size** box.

   - In the **Scaling** area, click **Fit to**. Then specify the number of pages horizontally and vertically across which you want to print the worksheet.

3. In the **Page Setup** dialog box, click **OK**.

Print sheet elements

When printing worksheet content, you have the option of printing some of the non-content elements that support the content, including the gridlines, row headings (the numbers on the left side of the sheet), column headings (the letters at the top of the sheet), comments, and cell error messages. Gridlines and row and column headings print as they look in the worksheet. You can choose to print comments in their actual locations or group them at the end of the sheet. You can print errors as they appear on the worksheet, delete them, or replace them with -- or #N/A.

If your worksheet contains multiple pages of tabular content, it will likely be helpful to readers to have the table column and row headings repeated on the top and left side of each page. You can designate the specific columns and rows to use for this purpose.

Numbers and letters   Titles in worksheet content

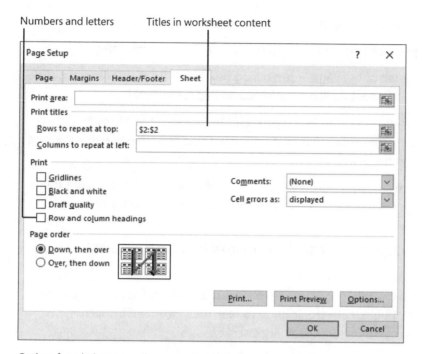

Options for printing supporting content and tabular content headers

To print supporting content

1. On the **Page Layout** tab, in the **Page Setup** group, click **Print Titles**.

2. On the **Sheet** tab of the **Page Setup** dialog box, in the **Print** section, do any of the following:

    -   Select the **Gridlines** check box to print the gridlines.

    -   Select the **Row and column headings** check box to print the row numbers and column letters.

    -   In the **Comments** list, click **At end of sheet** or **As displayed on sheet** to print cell comments in that location.

    -   In the **Cell errors as** list, click **displayed**, **--**, or **#N/A** to print the errors as specified, or click **<blank>** to hide the errors.

3. Click **Print Preview** to review the results of your selections, **Print** to print the worksheet, or **OK** to save the selections and return to the worksheet.

To display repeating row and column titles on multipage worksheets

1. On the **Page Layout** tab, in the **Page Setup** group, click **Print Titles**.

2. On the **Sheet** tab of the **Page Setup** dialog box, in the **Print titles** section, click in the **Rows To Repeat At Top** or **Columns To Repeat At Left** box.

3. In the worksheet, select the row(s) you want to repeat at the top of each page or the column(s) you want to repeat on the left side of each page, to enter that information in the dialog box.

4. Click **Print Preview** to review the results of your selections, **Print** to print the worksheet, or **OK** to save the selections and return to the worksheet.

Inspect a workbook for hidden properties or personal information

Excel includes three tools that you can use to inspect a workbook for possible problems before you distribute it electronically (as a file): the Document Inspector, the Accessibility Checker, and the Compatibility Checker.

The Document Inspector checks for content and information that you might not want to share with readers, such as:

- Information that identifies the document authors
- Comments and ink annotations
- Worksheets, rows, columns and names that are hidden; PivotTables, PivotCharts, cube formulas, slicers, and timelines that might include data that isn't visible; embedded data, files, and file links; and objects that have been formatted as invisible
- Page headers and footers
- Content add-ins and Task Pane add-ins that are saved in the workbook

- Real-time data functions that can pull external data into the workbook
- Excel Survey questions, defined scenarios, and content filters
- Macros, form controls, and ActiveX controls saved as part of the workbook
- Workbook and server properties

The Document Inspector offers to remove content that it locates, but doesn't provide specifics. You can opt to remove or retain any category of content. There are some types of content that you might want to keep and review individually.

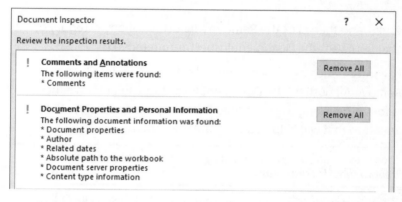
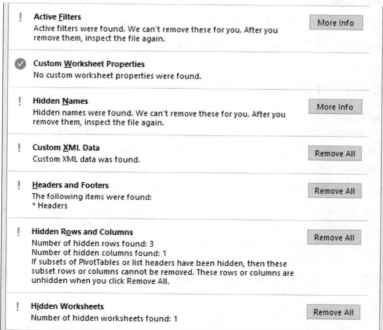

Some of the results reported by the Document Inspector

To inspect a workbook for common issues

1. Save the workbook, and then display the **Info** page of the Backstage view.

2. In the **Inspect Workbook** area of the **Info** page, click the **Check for Issues** button, and then click **Inspect Document** to open the Document Inspector dialog box, which lists the items that will be checked.

3. Clear the check boxes for any groups of properties you don't want to check for, and then click **Inspect** to display a report on the presence of the properties you selected.

4. Review the results, and then click the **Remove All** button for any category of information that you want the Document Inspector to remove for you.

   Some types of content, such as hidden names, display a More Info button instead of a Remove All button. The Document Inspector can't remove these content types for you; clicking the More Info button opens a webpage that provides information that will help you to locate the content.

   Tip You can choose to retain content identified by the Document Inspector if you know that it is appropriate for distribution.

   ---

5. In the **Document Inspector** dialog box, click **Reinspect**, and then click **Inspect** to verify the removal of the properties and other data you selected.

6. When you're satisfied with the results, close the **Document Inspector** dialog box.

Inspect a workbook for accessibility issues

The Accessibility Checker identifies workbook elements and formatting that might be difficult for people with certain kinds of disabilities to read or for assistive devices such as screen readers to access. These issues are divided by decreasing severity into three classifications: Errors, Warnings, and Tips. In Excel workbooks, the Accessibility Checker inspects content to ensure that it meets the criteria shown in the following table.

Error rules	Warning rules	Tip rules
▪ All non-text content has alternative text ▪ Tables specify column header information	▪ Hyperlink text is meaningful ▪ Table has a simple structure ▪ Tables don't use blank cells for formatting ▪ Sheet tabs have meaningful names	▪ Closed captions are included for inserted audio and video

See Also For detailed information about these and other Accessibility Checker rules, go to *https://support.office.microsoft.com/en-us/article/Rules-used-by-the-Accessibility-Checker-651e08f2-0fc3-4e10-aaca-74b4a67101c1* (or go to *support.office.microsoft.com* and search for "Accessibility Checker rules"). For more information about designing documents for accessibility, display the Accessibility Checker pane, and then at the bottom of the pane, click the Read More link.

From the Accessibility Checker pane, you can select any issue to display information about why it might be a problem and how to fix it. You can leave the Accessibility Checker open while you work—its contents will automatically update to indicate the current issues.

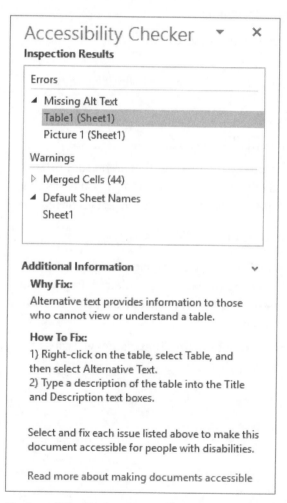

The Accessibility Checker pane provides direct links to possible issues

---

Tip After you run the Accessibility Checker, information about workbook content issues is also shown in the Inspect Workbook area of the Info page of the Backstage view.

To inspect a workbook for accessibility issues

1. On the **Info** page of the Backstage view, click the **Check for Issues** button, and then click **Check Accessibility** to run the Accessibility Checker.

2. In the **Accessibility Checker** pane, review the inspection results and make any changes you want to the workbook.

3. When you are done, do either of the following:

   - Click the **X** in the upper-right corner of the **Accessibility Checker** pane to close the pane.

   - Leave the pane open to continue checking for accessibility issues as you work with the workbook.

Inspect a workbook for compatibility issues

The Compatibility Checker identifies formatting and features that aren't supported or won't work as expected in Excel 2010 and earlier versions. Fixing these issues ensures that the appearance and functionality of the workbook will be consistent for all readers.

The Compatibility Checker has two categories of issues:

- **Issues that cause a minor loss of fidelity** These issues might or might not have to be resolved before you continue saving the workbook—data or functionality is not lost, but the workbook might not look or work exactly the same way when you open it in an earlier version of Excel.

- **Issues that cause a significant loss of functionality** These issues will cause the workbook to lose data or functionality.

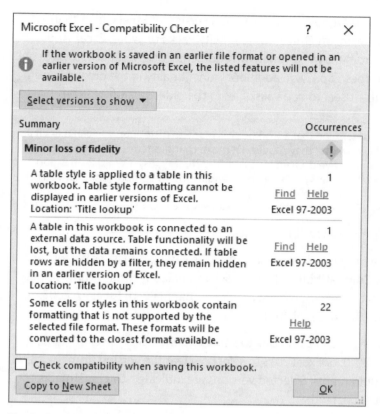

The Compatibility Checker provides information about possible issues

The following table identifies worksheet content and features that aren't compatible with some earlier versions of Excel (notably Excel 97-2003).

Minor loss of fidelity	Significant loss of functionality
• Color formatting in header and footer text • Even page or first page headers and footers • Unsupported cell formatting and style options (such as special effects and shadows) • More than 4,000 unique cell formatting combinations • More than 512 unique font formats	• Sparklines • More than 256 columns or 65,536 rows of data, or data scenarios that reference cells outside these limits • Custom international calendar formats • Specific non-Western calendar formats (such as Thai Buddhist or Arabic Hirji) • More than 64,000 cell blocks of data • Other features not supported prior to Excel 97-2003

If you share workbooks with people who are using a version of Excel earlier than 2007, they can install the free Microsoft Office Compatibility Pack For Word, Excel, And PowerPoint File Formats from the Microsoft Download Center at *download.microsoft.com*. The Compatibility Pack doesn't provide additional functionality in the older program version, but it does enable users to open .xlsx files in the older version of Excel.

><><><><><><><><><><><><><><><><><><><><><><><><><><><><><><><><><><><><><><><><><><><><><><><><><>

Exam Strategy After you determine that a workbook is ready to distribute, you can mark it as final, so that other people know that they should not make changes to it. Marking a document as final is part of the objective domain for Exam 77-726, "Microsoft Word 2016 Expert." The Microsoft Office Specialist exams for Excel don't require you to demonstrate that you can mark a workbook as final.

><><><><><><><><><><><><><><><><><><><><><><><><><><><><><><><><><><><><><><><><><><><><><><><><><>

To inspect a workbook for compatibility issues

1. On the **Info** page of the Backstage view, click the **Check for Issues** button, and then click **Check Compatibility**. The window immediately displays any formatting or features in the workbook that aren't compatible with Excel 97-2003, Excel 2007, Excel 2010, or Excel 2013.

2. To refine the list, click **Select versions to show** and then click Excel 97-2003, Excel 2007, Excel 2010, or Excel 2013 to select or clear the version from the compatibility requirements. Selected versions are indicated by check marks preceding the version.

To correct compatibility issues

1. Review the issue description and note the number of instances of the issue within the workbook. Some issues include a Help link to additional information.

2. Locate the named element by searching or scanning the worksheets, and then remove or modify it to meet the compatibility requirements.

3. When you finish, click **OK** to close the Compatibility Checker.

To maintain backward compatibility with a previous version of Excel

1. When saving the document, choose the previous file format in the **Save as type** list.

2. In the **Microsoft Excel - Compatibility Checker** window, click **Continue** to convert the unsupported features.

Objective 1.5 practice tasks

The practice files for these tasks are located in the **MOSExcel2016\Objective1** practice file folder. The folder also contains a subfolder of result files that you can use to check your work.

➤ Open the **Excel_1-5a** workbook and do the following:

❑ On the **Sales by Category** worksheet, set the print area so that only cells A1:C42 print.

❑ Configure the page setup options to print the worksheet gridlines.

❑ Display the print preview of the worksheet to check your settings.

➤ Save the workbook. From the **Excel_1-5_Results** folder, open the **Excel_1-5_results** workbook. Compare the two workbooks to check your work. Then close the workbooks.

➤ Open the **Excel_1-5b** macro-enabled workbook and do the following:

❑ Enable macros.

❑ Save a copy of the workbook with the file name <u>MOS-Compatible</u> in a file format that can be viewed and worked on by a colleague who is using Excel 2003. Notice the features that aren't compatible with the new file format.

❑ Save a copy of the *MOS-Compatible* workbook with the file name <u>MOS-Template</u> in a file format that supports macros and can be used as the basis for other similar workbooks in the future.

➤ Close the open workbooks. You can check your results against the files in the **Excel_1-5_Results** folder.

Objective group 2
Manage data cells and ranges

The skills tested in this section of the Microsoft Office Specialist exam for Microsoft Excel 2016 relate to managing cells and cell content in worksheets. Specifically, the following objectives are associated with this set of skills:

2.1 Insert data in cells and ranges

2.2 Format cells and ranges

2.3 Summarize and organize data

Excel stores data in individual cells of the worksheets within a workbook. You can process or reference the data in each cell in many ways; either individually or in logical groups. An organized set of contiguous data is a *data range.* A data range can be as small as a list of dates, or as large as a multicolumn table that has thousands of rows of data.

You might populate a worksheet from scratch or by creating, reusing, or calculating data from other sources. You can perform various operations on data when pasting it into a worksheet, either to maintain the original state of the data or to change it. When creating data from scratch, you can quickly enter large amounts of data that follows a pattern by filling a numeric or alphanumeric data series. You can fill any of the default series that come with Excel or create a custom data series.

This chapter guides you in studying ways of working with the content and appearance of cells and the organization of data.

To complete the practice tasks in this chapter, you need the practice files contained in the **MOSExcel2016\Objective2** practice file folder. For more information, see "Download the practice files" in this book's introduction.

> **IMPORTANT** If you apply an Excel table format to a data range, it then becomes a table, which has additional functionality beyond that of a data range. Tables are discussed in Objective group 3, "Create tables." The functionality in this chapter explicitly pertains to data ranges that are not formatted as Excel tables.

Objective 2.1: Insert data in cells and ranges

The most basic method of inserting data in cells is by entering it manually. This section discusses methods of creating and reusing data to fill a worksheet.

Create data

When you create the structure of a data range, or a series of formulas, you can automate the process of completing data patterns (such as *January, February, March*) or copying calculations from one row or column to those adjacent. Automation saves time and can help prevent human errors.

You can quickly fill adjacent cells with data that continues a formula or a series of numbers, days, or dates, either manually from the Fill menu, or automatically by dragging the fill handle. When copying or filling data by using the Fill menu commands, you can set specific options in the Series dialog box for the pattern of the data sequence you want to create.

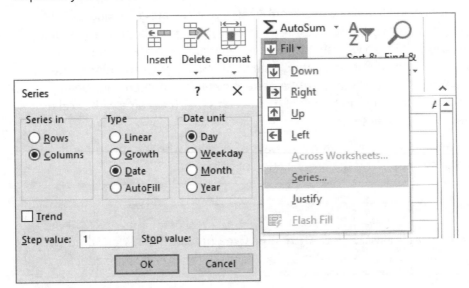

The Fill menu and Series dialog box

You can use the fill functionality to copy text data, numeric data, or cell formatting (such as text color, background color, and alignment) to adjacent cells.

When creating a series based on one or more selected cells (called *filling a series*), you can select from the following series types:

- **Linear** Excel calculates the series values by adding the value you enter in the Step Value box to each cell in the series.

- **Growth** Excel calculates the series values by multiplying each cell in the series by the step value.

- **Date** Excel calculates the series values by incrementing each cell in the series of dates, designated by the Date Unit you select, by the step value.

- **Auto Fill** This option creates a series that produces the same results as dragging the fill handle.

When you use the Auto Fill feature, either from the Fill menu or by dragging the fill handle, the Auto Fill Options button appears in the lower-right corner of the fill range. Clicking the button displays a menu of fill options. The fill options vary based on the type of content being filled.

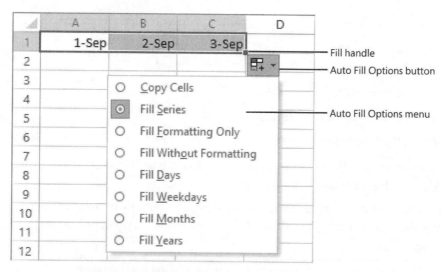

The Auto Fill Options menu when filling a date series

Tip The Auto Fill Options button does not appear when you copy data to adjacent cells.

You can use the Auto Fill feature to create sequences of numbers, days, and dates; to apply formatting from one cell to adjacent cells; or, if you use Excel for more sophisticated purposes, to create sequences of data generated by formulas, or custom sequences based on information you specify. You can also use the fill functionality to copy text or numeric data within the column or row.

If you want to fill a series of information that does not match the available series type or unit, you can create a custom fill series consisting of a specific list of data you want your series to conform to. For example, this could be a list of names, regions, or industry-specific reference points.

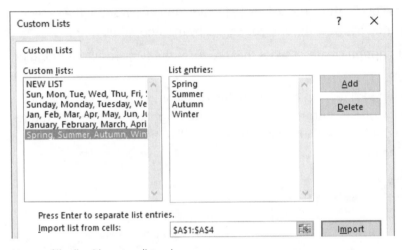

You can fill cells with custom list series

To fill a simple numeric, day, or date series

1. Do either of the following:

    - In the upper-left cell of the range you want to fill, enter the first number, day, or date of the series you want to create.

    - To create a series in which numbers or dates increment by more than one, enter the first two or more values of the series in the first cells of the range you want to fill.

    Tip Enter as many numbers or dates as are necessary to establish the series.

    ---

2. If creating a numeric series that has a specific number format (such as currency, percentage, or fraction), apply the number format you want from the **Number** group on the **Home** tab.

3. Select the cell or cells that define the series.

4. Do either of the following:

   - Drag the fill handle down or to the right to create an increasing series.

   - Drag the fill handle up or to the left to create a decreasing series.

   Tip When using the fill handle, you can drag in only one direction at a time; to fill a range of multiple columns and rows, first drag in one direction, then release the mouse button and drag the new fill handle in the other direction. The default fill series value is indicated in a tooltip as you drag.

   ---

5. If the series doesn't automatically fill correctly, click the **Auto Fill Options** button and then, on the **Auto Fill Options** menu, click **Fill Series**.

To fill a specific day or date series

1. Fill the series. Immediately after you release the mouse button, click the **Auto Fill Options** button that appears in the lower-right corner of the cell range.

2. On the **Auto Fill Options** menu, click **Fill Days**, **Fill Weekdays**, **Fill Months**, or **Fill Years**.

To set advanced options for a numeric, day, or date series

1. Enter the number or date beginning the series, and then select the cell range you want to fill.

2. On the **Home** tab, in the **Editing** group, in the **Fill** list, click **Series**.

3. In the **Series** dialog box, select the options you want, and then click **OK**.

To create a custom fill series

1. On the **Advanced** page of the **Excel Options** dialog box, in the **General** area, click the **Edit Custom Lists** button.

2. In the **Custom Lists** dialog box, enter the fill series elements in the **List entries** box, pressing **Enter** after each.

   Tip If the fill series elements are already entered on a worksheet, click the worksheet icon in the Import List From Cells box, select the fill series elements, click the icon again, and then click Import to add them to the List Entries box.

   ---

3. In the **List entries** list, verify or edit the entries. Click **Add**, and then click **OK** in each of the open dialog boxes.

To apply a custom fill series

→ Select a cell containing any entry from the custom list, and then drag the fill handle to create a series.

Tip Excel fills the series with either lowercase or capitalized entries to match the cell you start with.

To copy text or currency amounts to adjacent cells

1. In the upper-left cell of the range you want to fill, enter the text or currency amount (formatted as currency) you want to duplicate, and then select the cell.

2. Drag the fill handle up, down, to the left, or to the right to encompass the cell range you want to fill.

To copy numeric data to adjacent cells

1. In the upper-left cell of the range you want to fill, enter the value you want to duplicate, and then select the cell.

2. Drag the fill handle up, down, to the left, or to the right to encompass the cell range you want to fill.

Or

1. In the upper-left cell of the range you want to fill, enter the value you want to duplicate.

2. Select the source data cell and the entire cell range you want to duplicate the value into.

3. On the **Home** tab, in the **Editing** group, click the **Fill** button, and then in the list, click the first direction in which you want to duplicate the value (**Down** or **Right**).

4. To fill a cell range that includes multiple rows and columns, repeat steps 2 and 3, selecting the other direction.

Tip You can also fill a cell range up or to the left; if you do so, make sure that the value you want to duplicate is in the lower-right cell of the range you want to fill.

To exclude formatting when filling or copying data

1. Drag the fill handle to fill the series or copy the data, and then click the **Auto Fill Options** button.

2. On the **Auto Fill Options** menu, click **Fill Without Formatting**.

Reuse data

If the content you want to work with in Excel already exists elsewhere—such as in another worksheet or workbook or in a document—you can cut or copy the data from the source location to the Microsoft Office Clipboard and then paste it into the worksheet. If the content exists but not in the format that you need it, you might be able to reform the content to fit your needs by using the CONCAT function or the Flash Fill feature.

Cut, copy, or paste data

You can insert cut or copied cell contents into empty cells, or directly into an existing table or data range. Cutting, copying, and pasting content (including columns and rows) in a worksheet are basic tasks that, as a certification candidate, you should have extensive experience with. If you need a refresher on these subjects, see the Prerequisites section of the Exam Overview. This section contains information about Excel-specific pasting operations that you may be required to demonstrate to pass Exam 77-727 and become certified as a Microsoft Office Specialist for Excel 2016.

When pasting data, you have several options for inserting values, formulas, formatting, or links to the original source data into the new location. Paste options are available from the Paste menu, from the shortcut menu, and from the Paste Options menu that becomes temporarily available when you paste content.

2

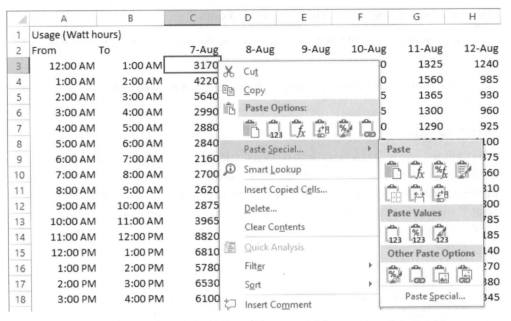

The available paste options vary based on the type and formatting of the content you're pasting

Excel also offers some advanced pasting techniques you can use to modify data while pasting it into a worksheet. By using the Paste Special feature, you can perform mathematical operations when you paste data over existing data, you can transpose columns to rows and rows to columns, and you can be selective about what you want to paste from the source cells.

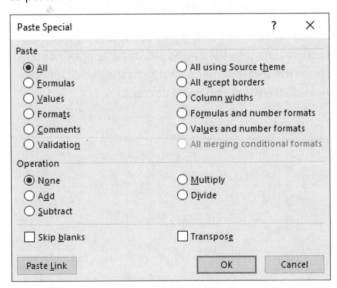

Paste specific aspects of copied content, or modify content while pasting it

You have the option to paste only values without formatting, formatting without values, formulas, comments, and other specific aspects of copied content. You can also link to data rather than inserting it, so that if the source data changes, the copied data will also change.

Paste options that are commonly used in business and that you should be comfortable with when taking Exam 77-727 include the following:

- **Pasting values** When you reuse a value that is the result of a formula, it is often necessary to paste only the value—the result of the formula—rather than the actual cell content.

- **Pasting formats** This is somewhat like using the Format Painter and can be useful when you want to build a structure on a worksheet that already exists elsewhere.

- **Transposing cells** Transposing content switches it from columns to rows or from rows to columns. This can be very useful when reusing content from one worksheet in another.

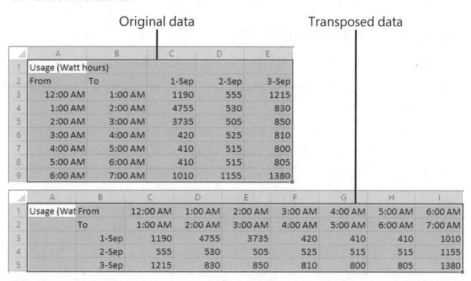

| | | Original data | | | Transposed data | | | |

▲	A	B	C	D	E			
1	Usage (Watt hours)							
2	From	To	1-Sep	2-Sep	3-Sep			
3	12:00 AM	1:00 AM	1190	555	1215			
4	1:00 AM	2:00 AM	4755	530	830			
5	2:00 AM	3:00 AM	3735	505	850			
6	3:00 AM	4:00 AM	420	525	810			
7	4:00 AM	5:00 AM	410	515	800			
8	5:00 AM	6:00 AM	410	515	805			
9	6:00 AM	7:00 AM	1010	1155	1380			

▲	A	B	C	D	E	F	G	H	I
1	Usage (Wat	From	12:00 AM	1:00 AM	2:00 AM	3:00 AM	4:00 AM	5:00 AM	6:00 AM
2		To	1:00 AM	2:00 AM	3:00 AM	4:00 AM	5:00 AM	6:00 AM	7:00 AM
3		1-Sep	1190	4755	3735	420	410	410	1010
4		2-Sep	555	530	505	525	515	515	1155
5		3-Sep	1215	830	850	810	800	805	1380

Excel transposes data very gracefully

Exam Strategy Be familiar with all of the Paste and Paste Special options, and know where to locate them.

To insert data into an existing data range

1. Select and copy the source content.

2. Select the upper-left cell of the range in which you want to insert the copied content.

3. On the **Home** tab, in the **Cells** group, click **Insert**, and then click **Insert Copied Cells**.

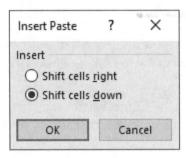

When inserting rows or columns

4. In the **Insert Paste** dialog box, click **Shift cells right** or **Shift cells down** to indicate the direction you want Excel to move the existing content.

To paste cell values (without formulas)

1. Select and copy the source content.

2. Do either of the following in the upper-left cell of the range to which you want to copy the values:

    • Select the cell. On the **Home** tab, in the **Clipboard** group, display the **Paste** list and then, in the **Paste Values** section, click the **Values** button.

    • Right-click the cell, and then in the **Paste Options** section of the shortcut menu, click the **Values** button.

To paste cell formatting (without content)

1. Select and copy the formatted source content.

2. Do either of the following in the upper-left cell of the range to which you want to copy the values:

    • Select the cell. On the **Home** tab, in the **Clipboard** group, display the **Paste** list and then, in the **Other Paste Options** section, click the **Formatting** button.

    • Right-click the cell, and then in the **Paste Options** section of the shortcut menu, click the **Formatting** button.

To transpose rows and columns

1. Select and copy the source content.

2. Do either of the following in the upper-left cell of the range to which you want to copy the transposed values:

   - Select the cell. On the **Home** tab, in the **Clipboard** group, display the **Paste** list and then, in the **Paste** section, click the **Transpose** button.

   - Right-click the cell, and then in the **Paste Options** section of the shortcut menu, click the **Transpose** button.

   Tip Transposing data retains its formatting.

Fill data based on an adjacent column

The Flash Fill feature looks for correlation between data that you enter in a column and the adjacent data. If it identifies a pattern of data entry based on the adjacent column, it fills the rest of the column to match the pattern. A common example of using Flash Fill is to divide full names in one column into separate columns of first and last names so you can reference them individually. (For example, when creating form letters.)

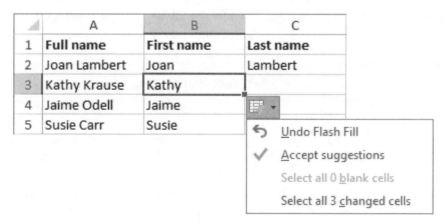

Flash Fill automatically fills cells with content from adjacent columns

To fill cells by using Flash Fill

1. In columns adjacent to the source content column, enter content in one or more cells to establish the pattern of content reuse.

2. Select the next cell below the cells that establish the pattern. (Do not select a range of cells.)

3. Do either of the following:

    *   On the **Home** tab, in the **Editing** group, click **Fill** and then click **Flash Fill**.

    *   Press **Ctrl+E**.

Tip If the Flash Fill operation doesn't work as intended, click the Flash Fill Options button that appears in the lower-right corner of the first filled cell and then, on the menu, click Undo Flash Fill. Enter content in additional cells to further establish the pattern, and then try again.

Replace data

The coverage of Objective 1.2, "Navigate in worksheets and workbooks," described methods of locating data and worksheet elements within a workbook. You can use similar methods to replace data within a worksheet. For example, you might reuse existing content by making a copy of a worksheet and updating the year within the worksheet formulas. You can replace content within the sheet or workbook in a single operation.

Unlike the Find operation, which you can use to search formulas, values, or comments, the Replace operation looks only in the cell content. It doesn't replace search strings in comments or in calculated values.

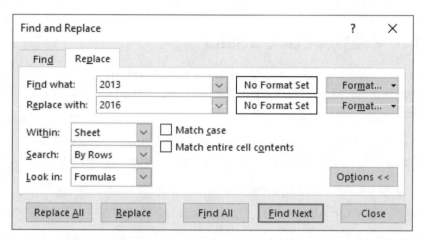

You can replace cell content throughout a worksheet or workbook

See Also For information about formulas, see Chapter 4, "Perform operations with formulas and functions."

To display the Replace tab of the Find And Replace dialog box

→ On the **Home** tab, in the **Editing** group, click **Find & Select**, and then click **Replace.**

→ Press **Ctrl+H.**

To replace data

1. On the **Replace** tab of the **Find and Replace** dialog box, enter the data you want to locate in the **Find what** box, and the replacement data in the **Replace with** box.

2. In the **Within** list, click **Workbook** or **Sheet** to set the scope of the operation.

3. Select the **Match case** or **Match entire cell contents** check boxes if necessary to further refine the search term.

4. Click **Replace All**, or click **Find Next** and then click **Replace** or **Find Next** for each instance of the search term that is located.

Objective 2.1 practice tasks

The practice files for these tasks are located in the **MOSExcel2016\ Objective2** practice file folder. The folder also contains a result file that you can use to check your work.

➤ Open the **Excel_2-1** workbook, and complete the following tasks by using the data in cells B4:G9 of the **Ad Buy Constraints** worksheet:

- ☐ Paste only the values and formatting into the range beginning at B18.
- ☐ Paste only the formulas into the range beginning at B25.
- ☐ Paste only the formatting (but not the content) into the range beginning at B32.
- ☐ Delete rows to move the headings to row 1.
- ☐ Delete columns to move the Magazine column to column A.
- ☐ Cut the data from the Mag3 row (B4:F4) and insert it into the Mag2 row (B3:F3).
- ☐ Move the *Cost Per Ad* data to the left of the Total Cost cells.
- ☐ Insert two blank cells in positions B8:B9, shifting any existing data down.
- ☐ Transpose the names in the Magazine column (cells A1:A6) to the first row of a new worksheet.

➤ On the **Price List** worksheet, do the following:

- ☐ Using the fill handle, fill cells A2:A21 with *Item 1, Item 2, Item 3*, and so on through *Item 20*.
- ☐ Fill cells B2:B21 with *10, 20, 30*, and so on through *200*.
- ☐ Fill cells C2:C21 with *$3.00, $2.95, $2.90*, and so on through *$2.05*.
- ☐ Copy the background and font formatting from cell A1 to cells A2:A21. Then delete the content of cell A1 (but not the cell).

➤ Save the **Excel_2-1** workbook. Open the **Excel_2-1_results** workbook, and compare the two workbooks to check your work. Then close the open workbooks.

Objective 2.2: Format cells and ranges

Merge cells

Worksheets that involve data at multiple hierarchical levels often use horizontal and vertical merged cells to clearly delineate relationships. With Excel, you have the following three merge options:

- **Merge & Center** This option merges the cells across the selected rows and columns, and centers the data from the first selected cell in the merged cell.

- **Merge Across** This option creates a separate merged cell for each row in the selection area, and maintains default alignment for the data type of the first cell of each row of the merged cells.

- **Merge Cells** This option merges the cells across the selected rows and columns, and maintains default alignment for the data type of the first cell of the merged cells.

In the case of Merge & Center and Merge Cells, data in selected cells other than the first is deleted. In the case of Merge Across, data in selected cells other than the first cell of each row is deleted.

Merged columns   Merged rows

	Monday		Tuesday		Wednesday		Thursday		Friday		
	15-Jul		16-Jul		17-Jul		18-Jul		19-Jul		
Time In		Total		Total		Total		Total		Total	Weekly
Time Out		0.0		0.0		0.0		0.0		0.0	Total
				Meal Break							
Time In		Total		Total		Total		Total		Total	
Time Out		0.0		0.0		0.0		0.0		0.0	
Total	0.0		0.0		0.0		0.0		0.0		0.0

Merging columns or rows retains the content of the first cell

To merge selected cells

→ On the **Home** tab, in the **Alignment** group, click the **Merge & Center** button to center and bottom-align the entry from the first cell.

→ On the **Home** tab, in the **Alignment** group, display the **Merge & Center** list, and then click **Merge Across** to create a separate merged cell on each selected row, maintaining the horizontal alignment of the data type in the first cell of each row.

→ On the **Home** tab, in the **Alignment** group, display the **Merge & Center** list, and then click **Merge Cells** to merge the entire selection, maintaining the horizontal alignment of the data type in the first cell.

Modify cell alignment, text wrapping, and indentation

Structural formatting can be applied to a cell, a row, a column, or the entire worksheet. However, some kinds of formatting can detract from the readability of a worksheet if they are applied haphazardly. The formatting you might typically apply to a row or column includes the following:

- **Text wrapping** By default, Excel does not wrap text in a cell. Instead, it allows the entry to overflow into the surrounding cells (to the right from a left-aligned cell, to the left from a right-aligned cell, and to both sides from a center-aligned cell) if those cells are empty, or it hides the part that won't fit if the cells contain content. To make the entire entry visible, you can allow the cell entry to wrap to multiple lines.

  Tip Wrapping text increases the height of the cell. Increasing the height of one cell increases the height of the entire row.

- **Alignment** You can specify a horizontal alignment (Left, Center, Right, Fill, Justify, Center Across Selection, and Distributed) and vertical alignment (Top, Center, Bottom, Justify, or Distributed) of a cell's contents. The defaults are Left and Top, but in many cases another alignment will be more appropriate.

- **Indentation** You can specify an indent distance from the left or right side when you choose those horizontal alignments, or from both sides when you choose a distributed horizontal alignment. A common reason for indenting cells is to create a list of subitems without using a second column.

- **Orientation** By default, entries are horizontal and read from left to right. You can rotate entries for special effect or to allow you to display more information on the screen or a printed page. This capability is particularly useful when you have long column headings above columns of short entries.

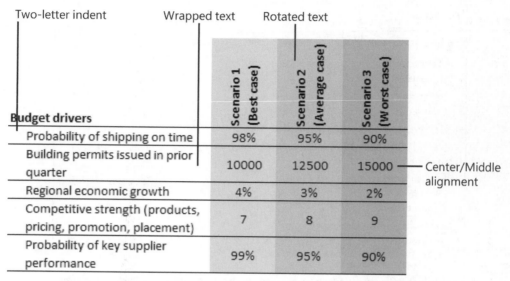

Structural cell formatting

Tip By default, row height is dynamic and increases to fit the text in its cells. If you manually change the height of a row and then change the size or amount of content in that row, you might have to set or reset the row height. For information about adjusting row height, see "Objective 1.3: Format worksheets and workbooks."

To wrap long entries in selected cells

➜ On the **Home** tab, in the **Alignment** group, click the **Wrap Text** button.

To align entries within selected cells

➜ On the **Home** tab, in the **Alignment** group, click the **Align Left**, **Center**, or **Align Right** button to specify horizontal alignment, or click the **Top Align**, **Middle Align**, or **Bottom Align** button to specify vertical alignment.

➜ On the **Home** tab, click the **Alignment** dialog box launcher. On the **Alignment** tab of the **Format Cells** dialog box, in the **Horizontal** and **Vertical** lists, click the cell alignment you want.

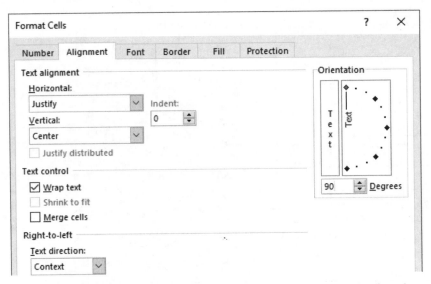

Configure text alignment, indents, orientation, and wrapping options at one time from the Format Cells dialog box

---

Tip Many more alignment options are available from the Format Cells dialog box than from the Format group of the Home tab.

To indent the content of selected cells

1. On the **Home** tab, click the **Alignment** dialog box launcher.

2. On the **Alignment** tab of the **Format Cells** dialog box, in the **Text alignment** section, do the following and then click **OK**:

    a. In the **Horizontal** list, select **Left (Indent)**, **Right (Indent)**, or **Distributed (Indent)**.

    b. In the **Indent** box, enter or select the number of characters by which you want to indent the text.

To change the orientation of the text in selected cells

→ On the **Home** tab, in the **Alignment** group, click the **Orientation** button, and then click the angle you want in the list.

Tip You can change the text alignment, text control, text direction, and text orientation settings on the Alignment tab of the Format Cells dialog box.

Apply cell formats and styles

By default, the font used for text in a new Excel worksheet is 11-point Calibri, but you can use the same techniques you would use in any Office 2016 program to change the font and the following font attributes:

- Size
- Style
- Color
- Underline

As a certification candidate, you should be very familiar with methods of applying character formatting from the Font group on the Home tab, from the Mini Toolbar, and from the Font and Fill tabs of the Format Cells dialog box.

Cell Styles are preconfigured sets of cell formats, some tied to the workbook theme colors and some with implied meanings. You can standardize formatting throughout workbooks by applying cell styles to content.

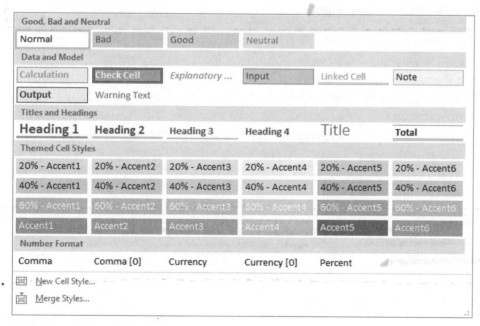

Some cell styles have specific meanings

To apply a cell style to a selected cell

1. On the **Home** tab, in the **Styles** group, click the **Cell Styles** button.

2. In the **Cell Styles** gallery, click the style you want.

Apply number formats

By default, all the cells in a new worksheet are assigned the General number format. When setting up or populating a worksheet, you assign to cells the number format that is most appropriate for the type of information they contain. The format determines not only how the information looks, but also how Excel can work with it.

You can assign a number format to a cell before or after you enter a number in it. You can also just start typing and have Excel intuit the format from what you type. (For example, if you enter *9/15*, Excel makes the educated guess that you're entering a date.) When you allow Excel to assign a number format, or you choose a format from the Number Format list in the Number group on the Home tab, Excel uses the default settings for that format. You can change the currency symbol and the number of decimal places shown directly from the Number group. You can change many other settings (such as changing the format of calendar dates from *15-Sep* to *September 15, 2016*) from the Format Cells dialog box.

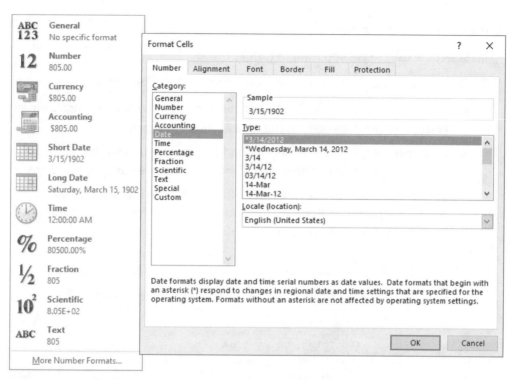

Select a data format that will provide clear information to workbook readers and fit the cell width you need

When you apply the Percent Style number format to a cell, the cell displays the percentage equivalent of the number. For example, the number 1 is shown as 100%, the number 5 as 500%, or the number 0.25 as 25%.

To apply a default number format to selected cells

→ On the **Home** tab, in the **Number** group, display the **Number Format** list, and then click a format.

Tip If you want a number to be treated as text, apply the Text number format.

To display the percentage equivalent of a number

1. Select the cell or cells you want to format.

2. Do either of the following:

   - On the **Home** tab, in the **Number** group, click the **Percent Style** button.
   - Press **Ctrl+Shift+%**.

To display a number as currency

1. Select the cell or cells you want to format.

2. On the **Home** tab, in the **Number** group, do one of the following:

    -   To format the number in the default currency, click the **Accounting Number Format** button (labeled with the default currency symbol).

    -   To format the number in dollars, pounds, euros, yen, or Swiss francs, click the **Accounting Number Format** arrow, and then click the currency you want.

    -   To format the number in a currency other than those listed, click the **Accounting Number Format** arrow, and then click **More Accounting Formats** to display the Accounting options.

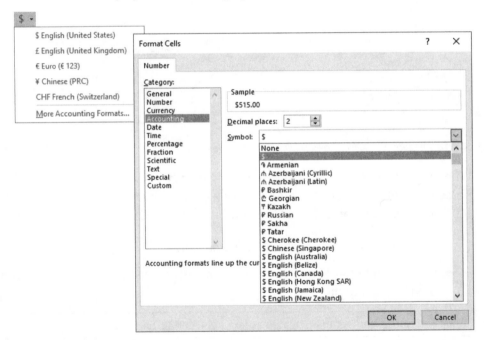

You can choose from hundreds of currencies

3. In the **Format Cells** dialog box, do the following, and then click **OK**:

    a. In the **Symbol** list, select the currency symbol you want to display.

    b. In the **Decimal places** box, enter or select the number of decimal places you want to display.

To display more or fewer decimal places for numbers

1. Select the cell or cells you want to format.

2. On the **Home** tab, in the **Number** group, do either of the following:

   - To display more decimal places, click the **Increase Decimal** button.

   - To display fewer (or no) decimal places, click the **Decrease Decimal** button.

To apply a number format with settings other than the default

1. Select the cell or cells you want to format.

2. On the **Home** tab, click the **Number** dialog box launcher.

3. On the **Number** tab of the **Format Cells** dialog box, select the type of number in the **Category** list.

4. Configure the settings that are specific to the number category, and then click **OK**.

Exam Strategy Exam 77-727 requires that you demonstrate the ability to apply built-in number formats. Creating and managing custom number formats is part of the objective domain for Exam 77-728, Microsoft Excel Expert.

Reapply existing formatting

If you apply a series of formats to one or more cells—for example, if you format cell content as 14-point, bold, centered, red text—and then want to apply the same combination of formatting to other cells, you can copy the formatting. You can use the fill functionality to copy formatting to adjacent content, or use the Format Painter to copy formatting anywhere. When using the Format Painter, you first copy existing formatting from one or more cells, and then paste the formatting to other cells. You can use the Format Painter to paste copied formatting only once or to remain active until you turn it off.

To copy existing formatting to other cells

1. Select the cell that has the formatting you want to copy.

2. On the **Mini Toolbar** or in the **Clipboard** group on the **Home** tab, click the **Format Painter** button once if you want to apply the copied formatting only once, or twice if you want to apply the copied formatting multiple times.

3. With the paintbrush-shaped cursor, click or select the cell or cells to which you want to apply the copied formatting.

4. If you clicked the **Format Painter** button twice, click or select additional cells you want to format. Then click the **Format Painter** button again, or press the **Esc** key, to turn off the Format Painter.

To fill formatting to adjacent cells

1. Select the cell that has the formatting you want to copy.

2. Drag the fill handle up, down, to the left, or to the right to encompass the cells you want to format.

3. On the **Auto Fill Options** menu, click **Fill Formatting Only**.

Objective 2.2 practice tasks

The practice files for these tasks are located in the **MOSExcel2016\ Objective2** practice file folder. The folder also contains a result file that you can use to check your work.

➤ Open the **Excel_2-2** workbook, display the **Employees** worksheet, and do the following:

❑ Merge cells A13:C14 so that the hyperlink is centered in a double-height cell across the three columns.

➤ On the **Expense Statement** worksheet, do the following:

❑ Select the entire worksheet and turn on text wrapping.

❑ Turn off text wrapping in only rows 4, 5, and 9.

❑ Right-align the entries in column A.

❑ Bottom-align the headings in row 9.

❑ Apply the *Angle Counterclockwise* orientation to the headings in row 9.

❑ Format cell K10 to display its contents as currency with a US dollar symbol and no decimal places. Then apply the same formatting to cells K11: K23.

❑ Apply the *20% - Accent2* cell style to cells A9:K9.

➤ Save the **Excel_2-2** workbook.

➤ Open the **Excel_2-2_results** workbook. Compare the two workbooks to check your work.

➤ Close the open workbooks.

Objective 2.3: Summarize and organize data

Format cells based on their content

You can make worksheet data easier to interpret by using conditional formatting to format cells based on their values. If a value meets a particular condition, Excel applies the formatting; if it doesn't, the formatting is not applied.

◢	A	B	C	D	E	F	G	H	I	J	K	L
1	Usage (Watt hours)											
2	From	To	1-Sep	2-Sep	3-Sep	4-Sep	5-Sep	6-Sep	7-Sep	8-Sep	9-Sep	10-Sep
3	12:00 AM	1:00 AM	1190	555	1215	585	1050	1960	1050	675	760	1870
4	1:00 AM	2:00 AM	4755	530	830	445	1190	2520	610	625	550	575
5	2:00 AM	3:00 AM	3735	505	850	485	585	1225	525	590	525	540
6	3:00 AM	4:00 AM	420	525	810	455	365	1160	450	555	550	555
7	4:00 AM	5:00 AM	410	515	800	530	390	795	450	670	540	540
8	5:00 AM	6:00 AM	410	515	805	820	375	785	440	545	530	560
9	6:00 AM	7:00 AM	1010	1155	1380	1085	365	790	435	565	535	545
10	7:00 AM	8:00 AM	1940	1980	2065	615	445	870	675	510	750	615
11	8:00 AM	9:00 AM	1870	1900	2090	455	435	925	770	755	760	615
12	9:00 AM	10:00 AM	1920	1955	2770	1605	1630	2765	1790	2085	2065	1790
13	10:00 AM	11:00 AM	1895	1845	2840	1710	2055	2105	1745	1980	2305	1825
14	11:00 AM	12:00 PM	1835	1755	5230	1915	3160	2115	1815	2500	2135	1810

Color scales and other conditional formatting can make it easy to quickly identify data trends

You set up conditional formatting by specifying the condition, which is called a *formatting rule*. You can select from the following types of rules:

- **Highlight cells** Apply formatting to cells that contain data within a specified numeric range, contain specific text, or contain duplicate values.

- **Top/bottom** Apply formatting to cells that contain the highest or lowest values in a range.

- **Data bars** Fill a portion of each cell corresponding to the relationship of the cell's data to the rest of the data in the selected range.

- **Color scales** Fill each cell with a color point from a two-color or three-color gradient that corresponds to the relationship of the cell's data to the rest of the data in the selected range.

- **Icon sets** Insert an icon from a selected set that corresponds to the relationship of the cell's data to the rest of the data in the selected range.

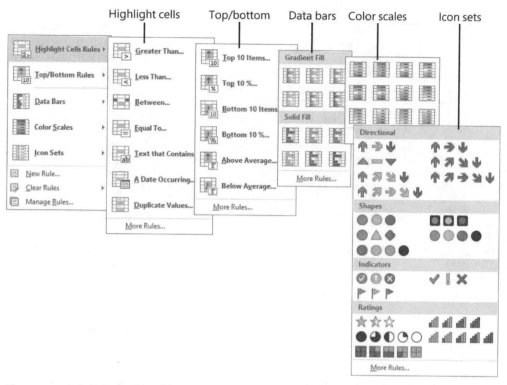

There are many built-in conditional formatting options

> **Exam Strategy** Familiarize yourself with the types of conditional formatting rules and their variations so that you know how to quickly apply any condition that might be requested on the exam. Exam 77-727 requires that you demonstrate the ability to apply built-in conditional formatting rules to static data. Creating custom conditional formatting rules and applying rules based on formula results are part of the objective domain for Exam 77-728, Microsoft Excel Expert.

To quickly apply the default value of a conditional formatting rule

1. Select the data range you want to format.

2. Click the **Quick Analysis** button that appears in the lower-right corner of the selection (or press **Ctrl+Q**) and then click **Data Bars**, **Color Scale**, **Icon Set**, **Greater Than**, or **Top 10%** to apply the default rule and formatting.

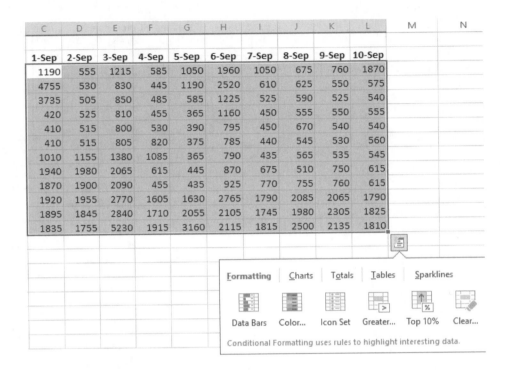

The Quick Analysis menu provides easy access to default conditional formatting

To format font color and cell fill in the selected data range based on a specified condition

1. On the **Home** tab, in the **Styles** group, click the **Conditional Formatting** button.

2. In the **Conditional Formatting** list, point to **Highlight Cell Rules** or **Top/Bottom Rules**, and then click the type of condition you want to specify.

3. In the dialog box, specify the parameters of the condition, click the formatting combination you want, and then click **OK**.

To apply formatting based on the relationship of values in the selected data range

→ In the **Conditional Formatting** list, point to **Data Bars**, **Color Scales**, or **Icon Sets**, and then click the formatting option you want.

To delete the conditional format applied to selected cells

→ In the **Conditional Formatting** list, point to **Clear Rules**, and then click **Clear Rules from Selected Cells** or **Clear Rules from Entire Sheet**.

→ Open the **Conditional Formatting Rules Manager** dialog box, click the rule, click **Delete Rule**, and then click **OK**.

Insert sparklines

Excel worksheets frequently contain vast quantities of numeric data that can be difficult to interpret. Excel provide a useful tool for adding a visual key to data that provides the user with information about how each entry within a data range relates to those around it: sparklines.

Sparklines are miniature charts that summarize worksheet data in a single cell. Excel 2016 includes three types of sparklines: Line, Column, and Win/Loss. Line and Column sparklines resemble charts of the same types. A Win/Loss sparkline indicates whether each data point is positive, zero, or negative.

	N	O	P	Q	R	S	T	U
1								
2	**12-Sep**	**13-Sep**	**14-Sep**	**15-Sep**	**16-Sep**	**17-Sep**	**18-Sep**	
3								
4	960	835	1245	395	1190	900	820	
5	1150	855	575	405	430	2475	465	
6	1020	785	385	400	430	1035	425	
7	505	835	350	395	425	460	430	
8	485	765	385	550	430	440	455	
9	495	800	395	470	430	450	420	
10	460	785	380	395	425	400	405	
11	645	875	550	2655	635	455	475	
12	690	3070	495	3670	1780	470	475	
13	1890	3770	1645	3865	2360	1575	1600	
14	1930	3150	1830	3735	2200	2195	1705	
15	1770	3155	1975	1900	3680	2100	1700	
16	1760	3100	1760	3125	2660	2955	1825	
17	1730	2695	1760	3650	2085	3800	1755	

Line sparklines (at the top) and column sparklines (on the side) help to identify data patterns

A sparkline consists of a series of markers. Depending on the sparkline type, you can choose to accentuate the first or last point in the data series, the high or low value, or the negative values, by displaying a marker of a different color. You can apply styles and other formatting to sparklines in the same way that you do to other graphic elements, by using commands on the Design tool tab that appears when a sparkline is selected.

Emphasize specific markers

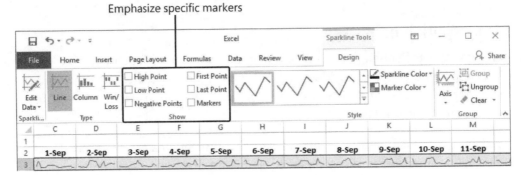

Sparkline colors are linked to the workbook theme

To create a sparkline or sparklines

1. Select the data you want to summarize, or click the cell in which you want to insert the sparkline.

2. On the **Insert** tab, in the **Sparklines** group, click **Line**, **Column**, or **Win/Loss** to specify the type of sparkline you want to create.

3. In the **Create Sparklines** dialog box, select, enter, or verify the data range and the location range. Then click **OK**.

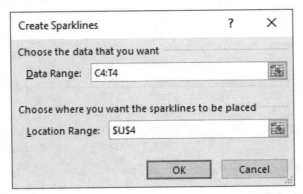

Create a sparkline in one cell and then copy it to others by using the fill feature

To enhance a selected sparkline

→ On the **Design** tool tab, do any of the following:

- In the **Show** group, select the check boxes for the data markers you want to show, and clear the check boxes for the data markers you want to hide.
- In the **Style** gallery, click the built-in style you want to apply.
- In the **Style** group, in the **Sparkline Color** gallery, click the color you want.
- In the **Style** group, in the **Marker Color** list, in the **Negative Points**, **Markers**, **High Point**, **Low Point**, **First Point**, and **Last Point** galleries, click the colors you want.

To change the type of a selected sparkline or sparkline group

→ On the **Design** tool tab, in the **Type** group, click the sparkline type you want.

To delete a sparkline or sparkline group

→ Select the sparkline you want to delete. On the **Design** tool tab, in the **Group** group, click the **Clear Selected Sparklines** button.

→ Select one or more sparklines in the sparkline group you want to delete. On the **Design** tool tab, in the **Group** group, click the **Clear Selected Sparklines** arrow, and then click **Clear Selected Sparkline Groups**.

Outline data and insert subtotals

You can designate specific rows or columns of data within a data range as groups. When you do so, Excel inserts a control, to the left of the row headings or above the column headings, with which you can contract and expand the data group. You can have column groups and row groups on the same worksheet, but you cannot have two consecutive groups of rows or columns; they must be separated by one row (the row can contain data). The grouping feature is particularly useful when you're working with a data range or table that is larger than your display, because it allows you to easily display and hide groups of columns and rows.

If your data range contains groups of data that are summarized or subtotaled, you can tell Excel to group the data into a maximum of eight levels. In effect, Excel outlines the data, making it possible to hide or display as much detail as you want. After grouping or outlining data, you can expand and collapse groups or levels.

Outline level selectors
Expanded group   Collapsed group

			A	B	C
1 2 3		1	**Name**	**Category**	**Sales**
		2	Blackberries	Berry bushes	31.50
		3	Gooseberries	Berry bushes	45.00
−		4		**Berry bushes Total**	76.50
		5	Anemone	Bulbs	112.00
		6	Autumn Crocus	Bulbs	75.00
		7	Begonias	Bulbs	37.90
		8	Bulb planter	Bulbs	13.90
		9	Daffodil	Bulbs	191.66
		10	Lilies	Bulbs	56.70
		11	Lily-of-the-Field	Bulbs	38.00
		12	Siberian Iris	Bulbs	69.93
−		13		**Bulbs Total**	595.09
+		17		**Flowers Total**	188.25
+		22		**Ground covers Total**	126.55
		23	Ambrosia	Herbs	50.00
		24	Anise	Herbs	11.30
		25	Beebalm	Herbs	16.50
		26	Chamomile	Herbs	4.25
		27	English Lavender	Herbs	24.75
		28	Lavender	Herbs	2.25
−		29		**Herbs Total**	109.05

Subtotals

Subtotaling creates groups that you can expand and collapse

Tip To outline by rows, you must ensure that each column has a heading in the first row. To outline by columns, you must ensure that each row has a heading in the first column. In either case, no row or column should be blank.

If your worksheet does not already have summary rows or columns, you can have Excel calculate the summary rows and outline the data in one operation, by using the Subtotal feature. The data range must include headers that identify data subsets, and must be sorted by at least one column that you want to use in the summary. You specify the way the data should be summarized in the Subtotal dialog box. You can use the SUM, COUNT, AVERAGE, MAX, MIN, PRODUCT, COUNT NUMBERS, STDDEV, STDDEVP, VAR, or VARP function to summarize the data of each subset of cells.

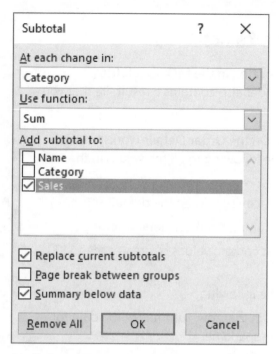

Specify the grouping, mathematical function, and columns to be calculated

After creating subtotals, you can use the controls that appear in the bar to the left of the row headings to collapse and expand subsets of data.

To create subtotals within a data range

1. Select the data range and sort it by the column containing the category of data you want to base the subset on.

2. On the **Data** tab, in the **Outline** group, click the **Subtotal** button.

3. In the **Subtotal** dialog box, verify that the correct subtotal category is shown in the **At each change in** list.

4. In the **Use function** list, click the summary function you want to use.

5. In the **Add subtotal to** box, select the check box of each column you want to add subtotals to.

6. Select the check boxes to replace current subtotals, present each data subset on its own page, or summarize the subtotals, and then click **OK**.

Objective 2.3 practice tasks

The practice files for these tasks are located in the **MOSExcel2016\ Objective2** practice file folder. The folder also contains a result file that you can use to check your work.

➤ Open the **Excel_2-3** workbook. On the **Order Details** worksheet, use conditional formatting to do the following to all the values in the Extended Price column:

- ❑ Apply the *3 Arrows (Colored)* icon set. (Keep the default settings.)
- ❑ Add blue data bars to the column. (Keep the default settings.)
- ❑ Fill all cells in the column that contain values of greater than $100 with bright yellow.

➤ On the **JanFeb** worksheet, do the following:

- ❑ Insert a row below the times. In that row, summarize the data for each hour by using a Column sparkline.
- ❑ Apply the *Colorful #4* sparkline style.
- ❑ Accentuate the First Point and Last Point data markers.

➤ On the **MarApr** worksheet, do the following:

- ❑ In column P, summarize the data for each day of March by using a Line sparkline.
- ❑ Apply the Sparkline Style *Accent 6, Darker 25%* style.
- ❑ Display all the data markers without placing emphasis on any specific type of data marker.

➤ On the **Sales By Region** worksheet, do the following:

- ❑ Subtotal the sales amounts by period.
- ❑ Undo the subtotals, sort the sales by region, and then use the Subtotal feature to display the average sales by region.

➤ Save the **Excel_2-3** workbook. Open the **Excel_2-3_results** workbook. Compare the two workbooks to check your work. Then close the open workbooks.

Objective group 3
Create tables

The skills tested in this section of the Microsoft Office Specialist exam for Microsoft Excel 2016 relate to creating tables. Specifically, the following objectives are associated with this set of skills:

3.1 Create and manage tables

3.2 Manage table styles and options

3.3 Filter and sort tables

Data stored in an Excel worksheet is organized in rows and columns of cells. Data in a contiguous range of cells is referred to as a *data range*. An Excel table is a named object that has functionality beyond that of a simple data range. Some table functionality, such as the ability to sort and filter on columns, is also available for data ranges. Useful table functionality that is not available for data ranges includes the automatic application of formatting, the automatic copying of formulas, and the ability to perform the following actions:

- Quickly insert column totals or other mathematical results.
- Search for the named table object.
- Expose the named table object in a web view.
- Reference the table or any table field by name in a formula.

This chapter guides you in studying methods of creating and modifying tables, applying functional table formatting, and filtering and sorting data that is stored in a table.

> To complete the practice tasks in this chapter, you need the practice files contained in the **MOSExcel2016\Objective3** practice file folder. For more information, see "Download the practice files" in this book's introduction.

Objective 3.1: Create and manage tables

Create an Excel table from a cell range

The simplest way to create a table is by converting an existing data range. If you don't already have a data range, you can create a blank table and then add data to populate the table.

When you create a table from an existing data range, you choose the table format you want, and then Excel evaluates the data range to identify the cells that are included in the table and any functional table elements such as table header rows.

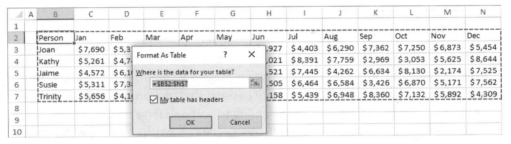

Excel evaluates the data range that contains the active cell

The table format you choose might have specific functional elements built in to it, such as a header or banded (alternating) row formatting. You can choose a format that has the options you want, or modify these and other table options after you create the table.

> **IMPORTANT** Names must begin with a letter or an underscore character. A name cannot begin with a number.

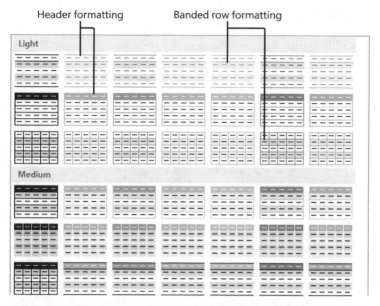

Choose from 60 preconfigured formatting combinations based on theme colors

Excel assigns a name to each table you create, based on its order of creation in the workbook (*Table1*, *Table2*, and so on). You can change the table name to one that makes it more easily identifiable (such as *Sales_2016*, *Students*, or *Products*).

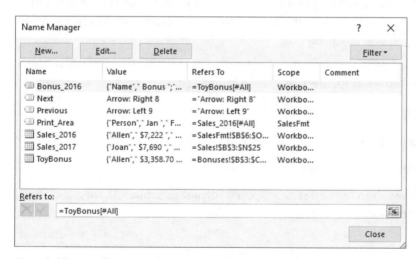

Named objects can be restricted to the scope of a single worksheet

To convert a data range to a table of the default style

1. Click anywhere in the data range.

2. On the **Insert** tab, in the **Tables** group, click **Table**. Excel selects the surrounding data and displays the Create Table dialog box.

Verify the table content

3. Verify that the cell range in the **Where is the data for your table** box is the cell range you want to convert to a table. If it isn't, do either of the following:

    -   Correct the cell range in the dialog box by changing the letters and numbers.

    -   Click the **Collapse dialog box** button to the right of the cell range, drag to select the cell range you want, and then click the **Expand dialog box** button to return to the full dialog box.

4. If you want to use the top row of the cell range as the table header row, verify that the **My table has headers** check box is selected.

5. In the **Create Table** dialog box, click **OK**.

To convert a data range to a table and select the table style

1. Click anywhere in the data range.

2. On the **Home** tab, in the **Styles** group, click **Format as Table**, and then click the table style you want.

3. In the **Format As Table** dialog box, do the following, and then click **OK**:

   a. Verify that the cell range in the **Where is the data for your table** box is the cell range you want to convert to a table. If it isn't, do either of the following:

      ○ Correct the cell range in the dialog box by changing the letters and numbers.

      ○ Click the **Collapse dialog box** button to the right of the cell range, drag to select the cell range you want, and then click the **Expand dialog box** button to return to the full dialog box.

   b. If you want to use the top row of the cell range as the table header row, verify that the **My table has headers** check box is selected.

To create an empty table

1. Select the cells in which you want to create the table.

   Tip If you select only one cell, Excel creates a two-cell table with one cell designated for the header and one for the content.
   ---

2. On the **Home** tab, in the **Styles** group, click **Format as Table**, and then click the table style you want.

3. In the **Format As Table** dialog box, click **OK**.

To select a table

→ In the worksheet, do either of the following:

   • Point to the upper-left corner of the table. When the pointer changes to a diagonal arrow, click once to select the table.

   • Drag to select all cells of the table.

→ Click the **Name** box located at the left end of the formula bar to display a list of named objects, and then click the table.

To change the name of a table

→ Select or click any cell in the table. On the **Design** tool tab, in the **Properties** group, click the table name to select it, and then enter the name you want to assign to the table.

Or

1. On the **Formulas** tab, in the **Defined Names** group, click **Name Manager**.

2. In the **Name Manager** window, click the table, and then click **Edit**.

3. In the **Edit Name** dialog box, select and replace the table name, and then click **OK**.

Add or remove table rows and columns

Inserting, deleting, or moving rows or columns in a table automatically updates the table formatting to gracefully include the new content. For example, adding a column to the right end of a table extends the formatting to that column, and inserting a row in the middle of a table that has banded rows updates the banding. You can modify the table element selections at any time.

To insert table rows and columns

→ To insert a column to the right end of a table, click in the cell to the right of the last header cell, enter a header for the new column, and then press **Enter**.

→ To insert a single column within a table, do either of the following:

- Click a cell to the left of which you want to insert a column. On the **Home** tab, in the **Cells** group, click the **Insert** arrow, and then click **Insert Table Columns to the Left**.

- Select a table column to the left of which you want to insert a column, and then in the **Cells** group, click the **Insert** button.

→ To insert multiple columns within a table, select the number of columns that you want to insert, and then in the **Cells** group, click the **Insert** button.

→ To insert a row at the bottom of the table, click in any cell in the row below the last table row, enter the text for that table cell, and then press **Tab**.

→ To insert a row within the table, do either of the following:

- Click a cell above which you want to insert a row. On the **Home** tab, in the **Cells** group, click the **Insert** arrow, and then click **Insert Table Rows Above**.

- Select a table row above which you want to insert a row (or select at least two contiguous cells in the row), and then in the **Cells** group, click the **Insert** button.

→ To insert multiple rows in a table, select the number of rows that you want to insert, and then in the **Cells** group, click the **Insert** button.

To move rows within a table

1. Select the table row or rows you want to move, and then do one of the following to cut the selection to the Microsoft Office Clipboard:

   - Press **Ctrl+X**.

   - Right-click the selection, and then click **Cut**.

   - On the **Home** tab, in the **Clipboard** group, click **Cut**.

2. Select the table row (or a cell in the row) above which you want to move the cut row or rows.

3. Do the following:

   - On the **Home** tab, in the **Cells** group, click the **Insert** arrow, and then click **Insert Cut Cells**.

Or

1. Select the worksheet row or rows containing the table row or rows you want to move, and then cut the selection to the Clipboard.

2. Select the worksheet row above which you want to move the cut row or rows.

3. Do the following:

   - On the **Home** tab, in the **Cells** group, click the **Insert** arrow, and then click **Insert Cut Cells**.

To move columns within a table

➜ Select the table column you want to move, and point to the top edge of the column. When the cursor changes to a four-headed arrow, drag the column to the new location (indicated by a thick vertical insertion bar).

Or

1. Select the worksheet column or columns containing the table column or columns you want to move, and then cut the selection to the Clipboard.

2. Select the worksheet column to the left of which you want to move the cut column or columns.

3. On the **Home** tab, in the **Cells** group, click the **Insert** arrow, and then click **Insert Cut Cells**.

To delete table rows and columns

→ Select one or more (contiguous) cells in each row or column you want to delete. On the **Home** tab, in the **Cells** group, click the **Delete** arrow, and then click **Delete Table Rows** or **Delete Table Columns**.

→ Right-click a cell in the row or column you want to delete, click **Delete**, and then click **Table Columns** or **Table Rows**.

Convert a table to a cell range

If you want to remove the table functionality from a table—for example, so you can work with functionality that is available only for data ranges and not for tables—you can easily convert a table to text. Simply converting the table doesn't remove any table formatting from the table. You can retain the formatting or clear it.

> **See Also** For information about applying and clearing table formatting, see "Objective 3.2: Manage table styles and options." For information about functionality that is specific to data ranges, see Chapter 2, "Manage data cells and ranges."

To convert a table to a data range

1. Do either of the following:

   • Right-click anywhere in the table, click **Table**, and then click **Convert to Range**.

   • Select or click any cell in the table. Then on the **Design** tool tab, in the **Tools** group, click **Convert to Range**.

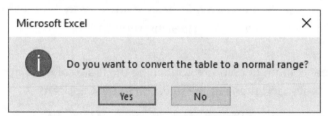

Converting a table removes functionality but not formatting

2. In the **Microsoft Excel** dialog box, click **Yes**.

Objective 3.1 practice tasks

The practice file for these tasks is located in the **MOSExcel2016\Objective3** practice file folder. The folder also contains a result file that you can use to check your work.

➤ Open the **Excel_3-1** workbook. On the **Sales** worksheet, do the following:

☐ Convert the data range A2:M23 to a table that includes a header row and uses the default table style.

☐ Assign the name Toys2016 to the table.

☐ Move the *July* column so that it is between the *June* and *August* columns.

☐ Move the *Linda*, *Max*, and *Nancy* rows at one time so that they are between the *Kay* and *Olivia* rows.

☐ Add a row to the table for a salesperson named Reina, between the *Quentin* and *Steve* rows.

☐ Add a row to the end of the table for a salesperson named William.

☐ Add a column named Dec to the right end of the table.

☐ Delete column M from the table.

➤ Save the **Excel_3-1** workbook.

➤ Open the **Excel_3-1_results** workbook. Compare the two workbooks to check your work.

➤ Close the open workbooks.

Objective 3.2:
Manage table styles and options

Apply styles to tables

When you create a table, you can apply a combination of formatting elements called a *table style*. The table style includes fonts, borders, and fills that are coordinated to provide a professional appearance. The available table styles are based on the worksheet theme colors. You can change the table style by choosing another from the Table Styles gallery.

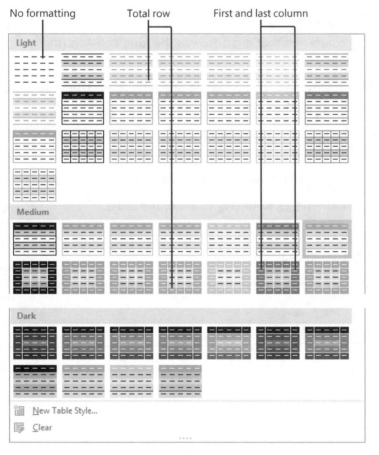

Excel modifies the styles based on the table options configured for the current table

To change the table style of the active table

1. On the **Design** tool tab, in the **Table Styles** group, do either of the following to expand the Table Styles menu:

    -   If the gallery is visible, click the **More** button.

    -   If the gallery is collapsed to a button, click the **Quick Styles** button.

2. In the **Table Styles** gallery, click the style you want.

To clear formatting from the active table

→   From the **Design** tool tab, expand the **Table Styles** menu, and then do either of the following:

    -   In the upper-left corner of the **Light** section of the gallery, click the **None** thumbnail.

    -   At the bottom of the menu, click **Clear**.

→   Select the table. On the **Home** tab, in the **Editing** group, click **Clear**, and then click **Clear Formats**.

Configure table style options

The table style governs the appearance of standard cells, special elements, and functional table elements, including the following:

-   **Header row** These cells across the top of the table are formatted to contrast with the table content, require an entry, and look like column titles, but are also used to reference fields in formulas.

-   **Total row** These cells across the bottom of the table are formatted to contrast with the table content. They do not require an entry, but clicking in any cell displays a list of functions for processing the numeric contents of the table column. These include Average, Count, Count Numbers, Max, Min, Sum, StdDev, and Var, and a link to the Insert Function dialog box from which any function can be inserted in the cell.

3

Table element formatting is designed to make table entries or fields easier to differen-
tiate, and include an emphasized first column, emphasized last column, banded rows,
and banded columns.

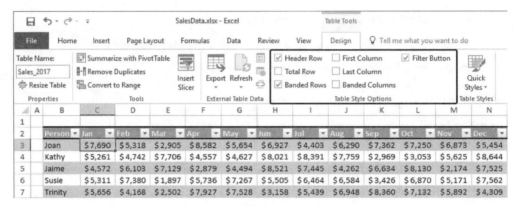

Configure formatting and functional options in the Table Style Options group

To enable table functionality in specific rows

→ On the **Design** tool tab, in the **Table Style Options** group, do any of the
following:

- To designate that the first row contains labels that identify the content
  below them, select the **Header Row** check box.

- To add a calculation row at the bottom of a table, select the **Total Row** check box.

- To hide or display filter buttons (arrow buttons) in the table header, clear or
  select the **Filter Button** check box.

Tip Excel automatically adds filter buttons when you format a data range as a table.
The filter buttons are adjacent to the right margin of each table header cell. If table
columns are sized to fit the column headers and you turn on filter buttons, the filter
buttons might overlap the table header text until you resize the column.

To apply contrasting formatting to specific table elements

→ On the **Design** tool tab, in the **Table Style Options** group, do any of the following:

- To alternate row cell fill colors, select the **Banded Rows** check box.

- To alternate column cell fill colors, select the **Banded Columns** check box.

- To emphasize the content of the first table column (for example, if the column contains labels), select the **First Column** check box.

- To emphasize the content of the last table column (for example, if the column contains total values), select the **Last Column** check box.

To configure the function of a Total row

1. In any cell, click the arrow to display the functions that can be performed in the cell.

22	Penny	$ 4,881	$ 5,021	$ 2,085	$ 3,521	$ 3,189
23	Brad	$ 1,814	$ 2,428	$ 1,592	$ 1,915	$ 1,523
24	Rob	$ 2,779	$ 2,111	$ 1,988	$ 1,715	$ 2,528
25	Madeline	$ 1,475	$ 1,506	$ 1,238	$ 1,792	$ 1,327
26	Total	▼				
27		None				
28		Average				
		Count				
29		Count Numbe				
		Max				
30		Min				
31		Sum				
		StdDev				
32		Var				
33		More Functior				

Modify a Total row to perform other mathematical functions

2. In the list, click the function you want to perform in the cell.

3. To perform the same function in all cells of the row, drag the fill handle to fill the rest of the row with the function.

Objective 3.2 practice tasks

The practice file for these tasks is located in the **MOSExcel2016\Objective3** practice file folder. The folder also contains a result file that you can use to check your work.

➤ Open the **Excel_3-2** workbook, on the **Sales** worksheet, do the following:

❏ Change the table style to *Table Style Medium 19*.

❏ Configure the table style options to format alternating rows with different fill colors.

❏ Configure the table style options to emphasize the first and last columns of the table.

❏ Add a total row to the table.

❏ Change the row name from *Total* to <u>Average</u>.

❏ Modify the cells in the row to calculate the average sales for each month and for the year.

➤ On the **Bonuses** worksheet, do the following:

❏ Remove the formatting from the table.

➤ Save the **Excel_3-2** workbook.

➤ Open the **Excel_3-2_results** workbook. Compare the two workbooks to check your work.

➤ Close the open workbooks.

Objective 3.3: Filter and sort tables

You can easily sort and filter content in an Excel table. Sorting sets the order of the content and filtering displays only rows containing entries that match the criteria you choose.

Filtered rows Active sort Sort and filter options Active filter

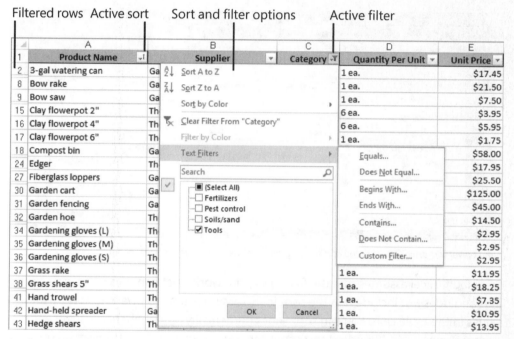

In a large data table, locate meaningful data by sorting and filtering the table content

Sort tables

You can sort or filter on one column at a time by using the commands on the menu that appears when you click the filter button at the top of the column, or you can configure a multilevel sort from the Sort dialog box.

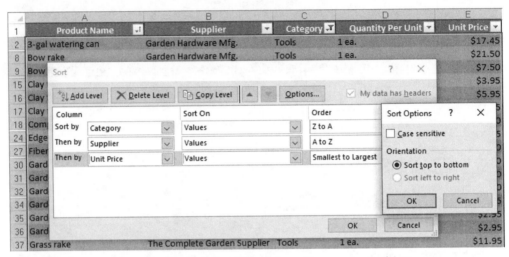

A multilevel sort provides a method of displaying different views of large amounts of data

By default, Excel assumes that the first row in the worksheet contains column headings and does not include it in the sort. It also assumes that you want to sort by the values in the table cells. You can sort values numerically or alphabetically in ascending or descending order. Standard sort orders are from A to Z for text, from smallest to largest for numbers, and from oldest to newest for dates. You can optionally sort by other features of the data range, including cell color, font color, and cell icon. These options are particularly useful in conjunction with conditional formatting.

You can also specify whether entries starting with uppercase and lowercase letters should be sorted separately and the orientation of the sort (whether you want to sort columns or rows).

Tip You can sort a table by the content of hidden columns within that table.

To sort a table by the values in one column

→ At the right end of the column header, click the filter button, and then click the sort order you want.

To sort the active table by multiple columns

1. Do either of the following:

    *   On the **Home** tab, in the **Editing** group, click the **Sort & Filter** button, and click **Custom Sort**.

    *   Click any cell in the range to be sorted, and then on the **Data** tab, in the **Sort & Filter** group, click the **Sort** button.

2. In the **Sort** dialog box, click the first column you want in the **Sort by** list. Then click the criteria by which you want to sort in the **Sort on** list. Finally, click the order you want in the **Order** list.

    Tip The options in the Sort dialog box change if you click Cell Color, Font Color, or Cell Icon in the Sort On list.

    ---

3. Click **Add Level**, and repeat step 2 for the second column. Repeat this step for additional columns.

4. Click **OK**.

To change the sort order

→ In the **Sort** dialog box, set the order for each of the sorting criteria.

→ In the table header, click the active sort button to reverse the sort order.

Filter tables

You can filter a table by the content of one or more columns. You can filter to include or exclude rows that contain an exact match of a column entry, that contain specific text, or that have a specific font color. Filters can include wildcards such as ? (a question mark) to represent any single character or * (an asterisk) to represent a series of characters.

To filter a table to match a specific column entry

1. Click the filter button in the header of the column by which you want to filter the table.

2. At the top of the list of column entries, clear the **(Select All)** check box, and then select the check boxes of the items you want to display. Then click **OK**.

    Tip You can enlarge the menu to display more options by dragging the handle in the lower-right corner of the menu.

To specify text filters

1. Click the filter button in the header of the column by which you want to filter the table, click **Text Filters**, and then click **Equals**, **Does Not Equal**, **Begins With**, **Ends With**, **Contains**, or **Does Not Contain**.

2. In the **Custom AutoFilter** dialog box, enter one or more filter criteria, and then click **OK**.

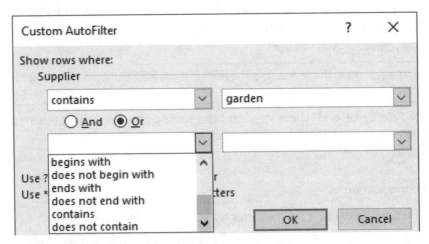

Custom filters can use two different criteria

To specify number filters

1. Click the filter button in the header of the column by which you want to filter the table, click **Number Filters**, and then click **Equals**, **Does Not Equal**, **Greater Than**, **Greater Than Or Equal To**, **Less Than**, **Less Than Or Equal To**, or **Between**.

2. In the **Custom AutoFilter** dialog box, enter one or more filter criteria, and then click **OK**.

To remove a filter

→ In the table header, click the filter button, and then click **Clear Filter From "*Column*"**.

To remove all filters from the active table

→ On the **Home** tab, in the **Editing** group, click **Sort & Filter**, and then click the active **Filter** command or click **Clear**.

→ Press **Ctrl+Shift+L**.

Remove duplicate table entries

When simplifying a table that contains many entries, or when compiling data from multiple sources, you might find that a table contains multiple matching entries. You can easily remove duplicate data from a table by using the Remove Duplicates feature.

Quickly cull duplicate rows from a table

Tip Use conditional formatting to locate duplicates so you can review them before permanently deleting them by using the Remove Duplicates feature. If you are uncertain about deleting the duplicate data, copy the original data to another worksheet as a backup.

To remove duplicate rows from the active table

1. On the **Design** tool tab, in the **Tools** group, click **Remove Duplicates**.

2. In the **Remove Duplicates** dialog box, select the columns in which you want Excel to look for duplicate entries. If you select multiple columns, Excel will remove only rows that contain duplicate entries in all the selected columns.

3. Click **OK** to remove the rows that contain duplicate entries in the selected columns.

Tip Remove any outlines or subtotals from your data before trying to remove duplicates.

Objective 3.3 practice tasks

The practice files for these tasks are located in the **MOSExcel2016\\ Objective3** practice file folder. The folder also contains a result file that you can use to check your work.

➤ Open the **Excel_3-3** workbook, display the **Bonuses** worksheet, and do the following:

❑ Apply a filter to display only the bonuses that were less than $2,500.00.

➤ Display the **Products** worksheet and do the following:

❑ Sort the data in ascending order by category and, within each category, by unit price.

❑ Sort the data in descending order by category and, within each category, alphabetically by product name.

❑ Remove duplicates so that there is only one entry for each supplier.

➤ Save the **Excel_3-3** workbook.

➤ Open the **Excel_3-3_results** workbook. Compare the two workbooks to check your work.

➤ Close the open workbooks.

Objective group 4

Perform operations with formulas and functions

The skills tested in this section of the Microsoft Office Specialist exam for Microsoft Excel 2016 relate to the application of functions and formulas. Specifically, the following objectives are associated with this set of skills:

4.1 Summarize data by using functions

4.2 Perform conditional operations by using functions

4.3 Format and modify text by using functions

Simple formulas and more complex functions provide the means to interpret raw data stored in a workbook in meaningful ways. They also provide a useful structure for processing information. You can increase the consistency and reliability of information by using formulas to calculate, evaluate, and express data.

You can calculate the data on a worksheet based on data in other areas of the workbook and in other workbooks. Excel maintains referential relationships when you move data or modify the data storage structure.

This chapter guides you in studying ways of referencing cells and ranges of cells both absolutely and relatively in formulas, and using formulas to sum and average cell values and count cells. It also guides you in processing data that meets specific conditions, and in manipulating text by using formulas.

> To complete the practice tasks in this chapter, you need the practice files contained in the **MOSExcel2016\Objective4** practice file folder. For more information, see "Download the practice files" in this book's introduction.

Objective 4.1:
Summarize data by using functions

Reference cells and cell ranges in formulas

Formulas in an Excel worksheet usually involve functions performed on the values contained in one or more other cells on the worksheet (or on another worksheet). A reference that you make in a formula to the contents of a worksheet cell is either a *relative reference*, an *absolute reference*, or a *mixed reference*. It is important to understand the difference and know which to use when creating a formula.

A relative reference to a cell takes the form *A1*. When you copy or fill a formula from the original cell to other cells, a relative reference changes to maintain the relationship between the cell containing the formula and the referenced cell. For example, copying a formula that refers to cell A1 one row down changes the A1 reference to A2; copying the formula one column to the right changes the A1 reference to B1.

An absolute reference takes the form *$A$1*; $A indicates an absolute reference to column A, and $1 indicates an absolute reference to row 1. When you copy or fill a formula from the original cell to other cells, an absolute reference will not change—regardless of the relationship to the referenced cell, the reference stays the same.

	A	B	C	D	E	F
1			Customer	Wingtip Toys		
2			Discount	20%		
3						
4	Product	Toy plane				
5	Base price	$ 15.00				
6						
7	Order quantity	Quantity discount	Price (each)	Order subtotal	Customer discount	Order total
8	100	0%	$ 15.00	$ 1,500.00	$ 300.00	$ 1,200.00
9	200	5%	$ 14.25	$ 2,850.00	$ 570.00	$ 2,280.00
10	300					
11	400					
12	500					

	A	B	C	D	E	F
1			Customer	Wingtip Toys		
2			Discount	0.2		
3						
4	Product	Toy plane				
5	Base price	15				
6						
7	Order quantity	Quantity discount	Price (each)	Order subtotal	Customer discount	Order total
8	100	0	=$B$5-($B$5*B8)	=A8*C8	=D8*$D$2	=D8-E8
9	200	0.05	=$B$5-($B$5*B9)	=A9*C9	=D9*$D$2	=D9-E9
10	300	0.075	=$B$5-($B$5*B10)	=A10*C10	=D10*$D$2	=D10-E10
11	400	0.1	=$B$5-($B$5*B11)	=A11*C11	=D11*$D$2	=D11-E11
12	500	0.125	=$B$5-($B$5*B12)	=A12*C12	=D12*$D$2	=D12-E12

The customer discount is calculated by using an absolute reference to the discount

A mixed reference refers absolutely to either the column or row and relatively to the other. The mixed reference *A$1* always refers to row 1, and *$A1* always refers to column A.

You can reference cells in other worksheets within the workbook. For example, you might prepare a Summary worksheet that displays results based on data tracked on other worksheets. References to cells on other worksheets can be relative, absolute, or mixed.

Tip You can reference a worksheet by whatever name appears on the worksheet tab.

You can also reference cells in other workbooks. For example, you might prepare a report that collates data from workbooks submitted by multiple regional managers.

When referencing a workbook located in a folder other than the one your active workbook is in, enter the path to the file along with the file name. If the path includes a non-alphabetical character (such as the backslash in C:\) in the file name, enclose the path in single quotation marks.

You can refer to the content of a range of adjacent cells. For example, you might use a formula to return the maximum value of all the cells in a row. When referencing a range of cells in a formula, the cell references can be relative, absolute, or mixed.

Drag to select cells   Formula bar   Color-coded cell references

C5	▾ ⋮	✕ ✓ ƒx	=SUM(C5:C11)	

	A	B	C	D	E
1	Category	Name	Sales	Category Subtotal	
2	Berry bushes	Blackberries	$31.50		
3	Berry bushes	Gooseberries	$45.00		
4				$76.50	
5	Bulbs	Anemone	$112.00		
6	Bulbs	Autumn crocus	$75.00		
7	Bulbs	Begonias	$37.90		
8	Bulbs	Daffodil	$13.90		
9	Bulbs	Lilies	$191.66		
10	Bulbs	Lily-of-the-Field	$56.70		
11	Bulbs	Siberian Iris	$38.00		
12				=SUM(C5:C11)	
13				SUM(**number1**, [number2], ...)	

Selecting one or more cells creates a relative reference

To insert a cell or range reference into a formula

1. In the cell or Formula Bar, position the cursor within the formula where you want to insert the reference.

2. Use the reference procedure that corresponds to the type of reference you want to insert.

To relatively reference the contents of a cell

→ Enter the column letter followed by the row number, like this:

A1

To relatively reference the contents of a range of cells

→ Enter the upper-left cell of the range and the lower-right cell of the range, separated by a colon, like this:

A1:B3

→ Drag to select the cell range and insert the cell range reference.

To absolutely reference the contents of a cell

→ Precede the column letter and row number by dollar signs, like this:

$A$1

→ Enter the relative reference, click in or select the reference, and then press **F4**.

To absolutely reference the contents of a range of cells

→ Enter the upper-left cell of the range and the lower-right cell of the range, separated by a colon, and precede each column letter and row number by dollar signs, like this:

$A$1:$B$3

→ Enter the relative range reference, select the range, and then press **F4**.

To reference a cell on a different worksheet in the same workbook

→ Enter the worksheet name and cell reference, separated by an exclamation point, like this:

Data!C2

Or

1. With the cursor in the formula, click the worksheet tab of the worksheet containing the cell you want to reference.

Tip You can watch the reference being built in the Formula Bar.

---

2. Click the cell or select the cell range you want to reference, and then press **Enter** to complete the cell reference in the formula and return to the original worksheet.

To reference a cell in another workbook

→ If the workbook is in the same folder, enter the workbook name in square brackets followed by the worksheet name and cell reference, separated by an exclamation point, like this:

[Sales.xlsx]Data!C2

→ If the workbook is in a different folder, enter the following, enclosed in single quotes: the path to the workbook, the workbook name in square brackets, and the worksheet name. Then enter an exclamation point followed by the cell reference, like this:

='C:\Projects\MOSExcel2016\[MyWorkbook.xlsx]MyWorksheet'!$A$1

Or

1. Open the workbook that contains the cell you want to reference, and then switch to the workbook you want to create the formula in.

2. With the cursor active where you want to insert the reference, switch to the second workbook, click the worksheet containing the cell you want to reference, click the cell or select the range you want to reference, and then press **Enter**.

Define order of operations

A formula can involve multiple types of calculations. Unless you specify another order of precedence, Excel evaluates formula content and process calculations in the following order:

1. **Reference operators** The colon (:), space ( ), and comma (,) symbols
2. **Negation** The negative (–) symbol in phrases such as –1
3. **Percentage** The percent (%) symbol
4. **Exponentiation** The raising to a power (^) symbol
5. **Multiplication and division** The multiply (*) and divide (/) symbols
6. **Addition and subtraction** The plus (+) and minus (-) symbols
7. **Concatenation** The ampersand (&) symbol connecting two strings of text
8. **Comparison** The equal (=), less than (<), and greater than (>) symbols and any combination thereof

If multiple calculations within a formula have the same precedence, Excel processes them in order from left to right.

You can change the order in which Excel processes the calculations within a formula by enclosing the calculations you want to perform first in parentheses. Similarly, when you use multiple calculations to represent one value in a formula, you can instruct Excel to process the calculations as a unit before incorporating the results of the calculation in the formula, by enclosing the calculations in parentheses.

The following table illustrates the effect of changing precedence within a simple formula.

Formula	Result
=1+2-3+4-5+6	5
=(1+2)-(3+4)-(5+6)	–15
=1+(2-3)+4-(5+6)	–7

To change the order of calculation within a formula

→ Enclose the calculations you want to perform first within parentheses.

→ Arrange calculations that have the same precedence in the order you want to perform them, from left to right.

Perform calculations by using functions

Formulas in Excel can be made up of values that you enter, values that you reference (cell references, named ranges, named objects), mathematical operators, and the functions that ultimately structure and control the formula. A function can be thought of as a service provided by Excel to do a specific task. That task might be to perform a mathematical operation, to make a decision based on specific factors, or to perform an action on some text. A function is always indicated by the function name followed by a set of parentheses (for example, the SUM() function). For most functions, arguments (variables) inside the parentheses either tell the function what to do or identify values for the function to work with. An argument can be a value that you enter, a cell reference, a range reference, a named range, a named object, or even another function. The number and type of arguments vary depending on which function you're using. It is important to understand the syntax of common functions and to be able to correctly enter the function arguments. Fortunately, you don't have to memorize anything; the Formula AutoComplete feature leads you through the process of selecting the correct function name and entering the required arguments in the correct syntax.

The following table describes the purpose of each of the functions that you can use to summarize data from a set of cells, and the types of arguments the functions accept.

Function	Purpose	Arguments
SUM()	Returns the total value of the cells	number1,number2,...,number255
COUNT()	Returns the number of cells that contain numeric values	value1,value2,...,value255
COUNTA()	Returns the number of cells that contain any content (are not empty)	value1,value2,...,value255
COUNTBLANK()	Returns the number of empty cells	range
AVERAGE()	Returns the average of the cell values	number1,number2,...,number255
MIN()	Returns the minimum value within the set	number1,number2,...,number255
MAX()	Returns the maximum value within the set	number1,number2,...,number255

4

Probably the most common formula used in Excel, and certainly the simplest to understand, is the SUM() function. The SUM() function returns the total value of a set of numbers. Rather than individually adding the values of all the cells you want to total, you can use the SUM function to perform this task.

Tip The results of the AVERAGE, COUNT, and SUM functions appear by default on the status bar when you select multiple cells (contiguous or separate) that contain numeric values. You can optionally display the Numerical Count, Minimum, and Maximum values.

Each of these functions takes up to 255 arguments, either numbers or values, as follows:

- An argument specified as a number can be a number that is entered directly in the formula, a text representation of a number (a number inside of quotation marks), a cell reference, a range reference, or a named reference. The function ignores any cells that contain text that can't be translated to a number, that are empty, or that contain an error.

- An argument specified as a value can be any type of value. For example, the COUNT() function will evaluate the specified cells and return the count of only those that contain values it identifies as numbers, whereas the COUNTA() function will evaluate the cells and return the count of those that contain any content (are not blank).

You can enter arguments directly in the formula structure, through a dialog box interface, by clicking to select cells, or by dragging to select ranges.

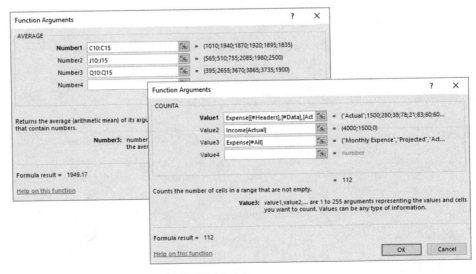

Arguments for the AVERAGE() and COUNTA() functions

To sum values

→ In the cell or formula bar, enter the following formula, including up to 255 numbers, which can be in the form of cell references, a data range, or specific numbers:

=SUM(number1,[number2],[number3]...)

→ On the **Formulas** tab, in the **Function Library** group, click the **AutoSum** arrow (not the button), and then click **Sum**. Select or enter the numeric arguments you want to sum, and then press **Enter**.

→ In the **Function Library** group, click the **AutoSum** button (not the arrow) and press **Enter** to accept the logical range of values selected by Excel (the range immediately above or to the left of the active cell).

→ Click the **AutoSum** button. Click or drag to select the input values you want (press and hold **Ctrl** to select multiple cells and ranges). Then press **Enter**.

Or

1. On the **Formulas** tab, in the **Function Library** group, click **Math & Trig**, and then click **SUM**.

2. In the **Function Arguments** dialog box, do the following, and then click **OK**:

   • In the **Number1** box, enter or select the first number.

   • In the **Number2** box and each subsequent box, enter or select the additional numbers up to a total of 255 arguments.

To count cells containing numeric values

→ In the cell or formula bar, enter the following formula, including up to 255 cell references or data ranges:

=COUNT(value1,[value2],[value3]...)

→ In the **Function Library** group, click the **AutoSum** arrow, and then click **Count Numbers**. Select or enter the cells you want to count, and then press **Enter**.

Or

1. In the **Function Library** group, click **More Functions**, click **Statistical**, and then click **COUNT**.

2. In the **Function Arguments** box, do the following, and then click **OK**.

   • In the **Value1** box, enter or select the first data range.

   • In the **Value2** box and each subsequent box, enter or select additional data ranges up to a total of 255 arguments.

To count non-empty cells

→ In the cell or formula bar, enter the following formula, including up to 255 cell references or data ranges:

=COUNTA(value1,[value2],[value3]...)

Or

1. In the **Function Library** group, click **More Functions**, click **Statistical**, and then click **COUNTA**.

2. In the **Function Arguments** box, do the following, and then click **OK**.

- In the **Value1** box, enter or select the first data range.

- In the **Value2** box and each subsequent box, enter or select additional data ranges up to a total of 255 arguments.

To count empty cells

→ In the cell or formula bar, enter the following formula, including up to 255 cell references or data ranges:

=COUNTBLANK(range)

Or

1. In the **Function Library** group, click **More Functions**, click **Statistical**, and then click **COUNTBLANK**.

2. In the **Function Arguments** box, enter or select the data range in the **Range** box, and then click **OK**.

To average values in a data range

→ In the cell or formula bar, enter the following formula, including up to 255 cell references or data ranges:

=AVERAGE(number1,[number2],[number3]...)

→ In the **Function Library** group, click the **AutoSum** arrow, and then click **Average**. Select or enter the cells you want to average, and then press **Enter**.

Or

1. In the **Function Library** group, click **More Functions**, click **Statistical**, and then click **AVERAGE**.

2. In the **Function Arguments** dialog box, do the following, and then click **OK**:

    -   In the **Number1** box, enter or select the first data range.

    -   In the **Number2** box and each subsequent box, enter or select additional data ranges up to a total of 255 arguments.

To return the lowest value in a data range

→ In the cell or formula bar, enter the following formula, including up to 255 cell references or data ranges:

  =MIN(number1,[number2],[number3]…)

→ In the **Function Library** group, click the **AutoSum** arrow, and then click **Min**. Select or enter the cells you want to evaluate, and then press **Enter**.

Or

1. In the **Function Library** group, click **More Functions**, click **Statistical**, and then click **MIN**.

2. In the **Function Arguments** dialog box, do the following, and then click **OK**:

    -   In the **Number1** box, enter or select the first data range.

    -   In the **Number2** box and each subsequent box, enter or select additional data ranges up to a total of 255 arguments.

To return the highest value in a data range

→ In the cell or formula bar, enter the following formula, including up to 255 cell references or data ranges:

  =MAX(number1,[number2],[number3]…)

→ In the **Function Library** group, click the **AutoSum** arrow, and then click **Max**. Select or enter the cells you want to evaluate, and then press **Enter**.

Or

1. In the **Function Library** group, click **More Functions**, click **Statistical**, and then click **MAX**.

2. In the **Function Arguments** dialog box, do the following, and then click **OK**:

    -   In the **Number1** box, enter or select the first data range.

    -   In the **Number2** box and each subsequent box, enter or select additional data ranges up to a total of 255 arguments.

4

Objective 4.1 practice tasks

The practice files for these tasks are located in the **MOSExcel2016\ Objective4** practice file folder. The folder also contains result files that you can use to check your work.

➤ Open the **Excel_4-1a** workbook and do the following:

- ❑ On the **Multiplication Table** worksheet, create a formula in cells B2:T20 to complete the multiplication table of the numbers 1 through 20.

- ❑ Save the **Excel_4-1a** workbook. Open the **Excel_4-1a_results** workbook, and compare the two workbooks to check your work. Then close the open workbooks.

➤ Open the **Excel_4-1b** workbook and do the following:

- ❑ On the **Summary** worksheet, display the total sales for each period in cells B2:B5 by referencing the corresponding worksheets.

- ❑ Save the **Excel_4-1b** workbook. Open the **Excel_4-1b_results** workbook, and compare the two workbooks to check your work. Then close the open workbooks.

➤ Open the **Excel_4-1c** workbook, display the **Seasonal** worksheet, and do the following:

- ❑ In cell B18, create a formula that returns the number of non-empty cells in the Period range.

- ❑ In cell C18, create a formula that returns the average value in the Sales range.

- ❑ In cell D5, create a formula that returns the lowest Sales value for the Fall period.

➤ On the **Sales By Category** worksheet, do the following:

❏ In cells C95, C101, and C104, calculate the sales total for each category by using a relative cell range reference.

❏ In cell C86, calculate the Cacti sales total, using an absolute cell range reference.

➤ On the **Sales By Region** worksheet, create formulas to do the following:

❏ Create subtotals of sales amounts first by *Period* and then by *Region*.

❏ Find the average sales by *Period* and then by *Region*.

❏ Find the maximum and minimum values by *Period* and then by *Region*.

➤ Save the **Excel_4-1c** workbook.

➤ Open the **Excel_4-1c_results** workbook. Compare the two workbooks to check your work.

➤ Close the open workbooks.

Objective 4.2: Perform conditional operations by using functions

You can use a formula to display specific results when certain conditions are met. To do so, you create a formula that uses conditional logic; specifically the IF() function or one of its variations shown in the following table.

Function	Description
SUMIF() SUMIFS()	Returns the sum of values in a range that meet one or more criteria
COUNTIF() COUNTIFS	Returns the number of cells in a range that meet one or more criteria
AVERAGEIF() AVERAGEIFS()	Returns the average of values in a range that meet one or more criteria

A formula that uses conditional logic evaluates a specific condition and then returns one of two results based on whether the logical test evaluates as TRUE or FALSE.

The correct syntax for the IF() function is *IF(logical_test,value_if_true,value_if_false)*. For example, the following formula evaluates a student's grade in cell D4 and returns Pass if the grade is 70 or above and Fail if the grade is less than 70:

   =IF(D4<70,"Fail","Pass")

When using the IF() function, the logical test must be one that can have only a true or false result.

Tip   The IF() function in Excel is equivalent to an IF...THEN...ELSE function in a computer program.

The logical test and the results can include text strings or calculations. Enclose text strings within the formula in quotation marks. When using a numeric value or calculation as a logical test, enclose it in quotation marks.

The syntax for the SUMIF function is *SUMIF(range,criteria,sum_range)*.

The syntax for the COUNTIF function is *COUNTIF(range,criteria)*. For example, the following formula returns the number of students within a table who are in grade 5:

=COUNTIF(AllGirls[[#All],[Grade]],"5")

The syntax for the AVERAGEIF function is *AVERAGEIF(range,criteria,average_range)*.

	▼	:	✕ ✓ *fx*	=COUNTIF(I:I,N12)				

	C	G	H	I	J	M	N	O	P
1	**OrderDate**	**Address**	**City**	**Region**	**PostalCode**		**Orders by Region**		
2	1/5/2016	991 S. Mississippi Rd.	St. Louis	MO	89203		Region	Quantity	
3	1/5/2016	8808 Backbay St.	Boston	MA	88337		BC	9	
4	1/6/2016	666 Fords Landing	Westover	WV	66954		CA	7	
5	1/6/2016	401 Rodeo Dr.	Auburn	WA	34923		ID	3	
6	1/8/2016	4568 Spaulding Ave. N.	Seattle	WA	12345		MA	1	
7	1/12/2016	14 S. Elm Dr.	Moscow	ID	02912		MO	1	
8	1/12/2016	12 Juanita Ln.	Helena	MT	42665		MT	2	
9	1/12/2016	78 Miller St.	Seattle	WA	81233		OR	4	
10	1/12/2016	27 Christopher St.	Seattle	WA	67645		Quebec	0	
11	1/13/2016	18 Elm St.	Tulalip	WA	77483		UT	1	
12	1/14/2016	511 Lincoln Ave.	Burns	OR	27182		WA	=COUNTIF(I:I,N12)	
13	1/14/2016	42 El Camino Dr.	Seattle	WA	11299				

You can reference a column in a formula by entering the column letter, a colon, and the same column letter

The criteria is a condition in the form of a number, expression, or text that defines which cells will be included in the calculation.

> **Exam Strategy** You can nest multiple functions so that Excel evaluates multiple conditions before returning a result. You can add logical tests to a conditional formula by using the AND(), OR(), and NOT() functions. Nested functions, the multiple-condition formulas SUMIFS(), COUNTIFS(), and AVERAGEIFS(), and custom conditional formats are part of the objective domain for Microsoft Office Specialist Exam 77-728, Microsoft Excel Expert.

4

To return a value based on a conditional test

→ In the cell or formula bar, enter the following formula, where *logical_test* is the condition that must be met, *value_if_true* is the value the formula returns if the condition is met, and *value_if_false* is the value the formula returns if the condition is not met:

= IF(logical_test, value_if_true, value_if_false)

Or

1. On the **Formulas** tab, in the **Function Library** group, click **Logical**, and then click **IF**.

2. In the **Function Arguments** dialog box, do the following, and then click **OK**:

   • In the **Logical_test** box, enter a pass/fail condition.

   • In the **Value_if_true** box, enter the value the formula will return if the condition is met. To return a text string, enclose it in quotes.

   • In the **Value_if_false** box, enter the value the formula will return if the condition is not met.

To sum values in a data range that meet a condition

→ In the cell or formula bar, enter the following formula, where *range* is the data range you want to evaluate, *criteria* is the condition that defines which cells will be summed, and *sum_range* is the data range within which cells will be summed:

=SUMIF(range, criteria, sum_range)

Or

1. On the **Formulas** tab, in the **Function Library** group, click **Math & Trig**, and then click **SUMIF**.

2. In the **Function Arguments** dialog box, do the following, and then click **OK**:

   • In the **Range** box, enter or select the data range you want to evaluate.

   • In the **Criteria** box, enter the condition, in the form of a number, expression, or text, that defines the cells that will be summed.

   • In the **Sum_range** box, enter or select the data range within which you want to sum qualifying cell values. If this argument is left blank, the formula sums cells within the data range in the **Range** box.

To count cells in a data range that meet a condition

→ In the cell or formula bar, enter the following formula, where *range* is the data range you want to evaluate and count, and *criteria* is the condition that defines which cells will be counted:

=COUNTIF(range,criteria)

Or

1. On the **Formulas** tab, in the **Function Library** group, click **More Functions**, click **Statistical**, and then click **COUNTIF**.

2. In the **Function Arguments** dialog box, do the following, and then click **OK**:

   - In the **Range** box, enter or select the data range you want to evaluate.

   - In the **Criteria** box, enter the condition, in the form of a number, expression, or text, that defines the cells that will be counted.

To average values in a data range that meet a condition

→ In the cell or formula bar, enter the following formula, where *range* is the data range you want to evaluate, *criteria* is the condition that defines which cells will be averaged, and *average_range* is the data range within which cells will be averaged:

=AVERAGEIF(range,criteria,average_range)

Or

1. On the **Formulas** tab, in the **Function Library** group, click **More Functions**, click **Statistical**, and then click **AVERAGEIF**.

2. In the **Function Arguments** dialog box, do the following, and then click **OK**:

   - In the **Range** box, enter or select the data range you want to evaluate.

   - In the **Criteria** box, enter the condition, in the form of a number, expression, or text, that defines the cells that will be averaged.

   - In the **Average_range** box, enter or select the data range within which you want to average qualifying cell values. If left blank, the formula averages cells within the data range in the Range box.

4

Objective 4.2 practice tasks

The practice file for these tasks is located in the **MOSExcel2016\Objective4** practice file folder. The folder also contains a result file that you can use to check your work.

➤ Open the **Excel_4-2** workbook. On the **Expense Statement** worksheet, do the following:

❑ Select cell C25 and review the formula, which uses the AND function to determine whether the Entertainment total is less than or equal to $200.00 *and* the Misc. total is less than or equal to $100.00.

❑ Select cell C26 and review the formula, which uses the OR function to determine whether the Entertainment total is more than $200.00 *or* the Misc. total is more than $100.00.

❑ In cell C27, use the IF function to display the text "Expenses are okay" if C25 evaluates to TRUE and "Expenses are too high" if C25 evaluates to FALSE.

❑ In cell C28, use the IF function to display the text "Expenses are okay" if C26 evaluates to NOT TRUE and "Expenses are too high" if C26 evaluates to NOT FALSE.

❑ To check your work, increase the Entertainment expenses by entering <u>100</u> in cell H13.

❑ In cell G28, use the COUNTIF function to return the number of cells in the range D10:I19 that contain values greater than zero.

➤ Save the **Excel_4-2** workbook.

➤ Open the **Excel_4-2_results** workbook. Compare the two workbooks to check your work.

➤ Close the open workbooks.

Objective 4.3: Format and modify text by using functions

You can use the formulas shown in the following table to return text strings.

Function	Description
LEFT()	Returns the leftmost character or characters of a text string
MID()	Returns a specific number of characters from a text string, starting at the position you specify
RIGHT()	Returns the rightmost character or characters of a text string
UPPER()	Converts text to uppercase
LOWER()	Converts text to lowercase
PROPER()	Capitalizes the first letter of each word in a text string
CONCAT()	Concatenates up to 255 text components into one string

> **IMPORTANT** The CONCATENATE() function that was available in earlier versions of Excel has been replaced in Excel 2016 by the CONCAT() function. CONCATENATE() is available in Excel 2016 for backward compatibility, but might not be available in future versions of Excel.

The LEFT(), MID(), and RIGHT() functions count each character in the specified text string. The LEFT() and RIGHT() functions take the following arguments:

- **text** (required) The text string to be evaluated by the formula.
- **num_chars** (optional) The number of characters to be returned. If *num_chars* is not specified, the function returns one character.

The syntax for the LEFT() and RIGHT() functions is:

LEFT(text,num_chars)

RIGHT(text,num_chars)

For example, the formula *=LEFT(Students[@[Last Name]],1)* returns the first letter of the student's last name.

The MID() function takes the following arguments:

- **text** (required) The text string to be evaluated by the formula.
- **start_num** (required) The position from the left of the first character you want to extract. If *start_num* is greater than the number of characters in the text string, the function returns an empty string.
- **num_chars** (required) The number of characters to be returned. If *num_chars* is not specified, the function returns one character.

The syntax for the MID() function is:

MID(text,start_num,num_chars)

| COUNTA | ▾ | ⋮ | ✕ | ✓ | *fx* | =MID(A2,5,8) |

◢	A	B	C	D
1	**Phone**	**Area code**	**Local number**	
2	817-555-0100	817	=MID(A2,5,8)	
3	972-555-0134	972	555-0134	
4	425-555-0158	425	555-0158	
5	360-555-0194	360	555-0194	
6	123-555-0167	123	555-0167	

The MID() function returns a specific number of characters from a text string

The UPPER(), LOWER(), and PROPER() functions each take only one argument: the text string to be processed. The syntax of the functions is:

UPPER(text)

LOWER(text)

PROPER(text)

The CONCAT() function can be very useful when working with text data. Using this function, you can merge existing content from cells in addition to content that you enter in the formula. The syntax for the CONCAT() function is:

CONCAT(text1, [text2], ...)

For example, this formula returns a result such as *Smith, John: Grade 5*.

=CONCAT(Table1[@[Last Name]],", ",Table1[@[First Name]],": Grade ",Table1[@Grade])

Tip You can use the ampersand (&) operator to perform the same process as the CONCAT() function. For example, =A1&B1 returns the same value as =CONCAT(A1,B1).

To return one or more characters from the left end of a text string

→ In the cell or formula bar, enter the following formula, where *text* is the source text and *num_chars* is the number of characters you want to return:

=LEFT(text,num_chars)

Or

1. On the **Formulas** tab, in the **Function Library** group, click **Text**, and then click **LEFT**.

2. In the **Function Arguments** dialog box, do the following, and then click **OK**:

   • In the **Text** box, enter or select the source text.

   • In the **Num_chars** box, enter the number of characters you want to return.

To return one or more characters from within a text string

→ In the cell or formula bar, enter the following formula, where *text* is the source text, *start_num* is the character from which you want to begin returning characters, and *num_chars* is the number of characters you want to return:

=MID(text,start_num,num_chars)

Or

1. On the **Formulas** tab, in the **Function Library** group, click **Text**, and then click **MID**.

2. In the **Function Arguments** dialog box, do the following, and then click **OK**:

   • In the **Text** box, enter or select the source text.

   • In the **Start_num** box, enter the character from which you want to begin returning characters.

   • In the **Num_chars** box, enter the number of characters you want to return.

4

To return one or more characters from the right end of a text string

→ In the cell or formula bar, enter the following formula, where *text* is the source text and *num_chars* is the number of characters you want to return:

=RIGHT(text,num_chars)

Or

1. On the **Formulas** tab, in the **Function Library** group, click **Text**, and then click **RIGHT**.

2. In the **Function Arguments** dialog box, do the following, and then click **OK**:

   • In the **Text** box, enter or select the source text.

   • In the **Num_chars** box, enter the number of characters you want to return.

To convert a text string to uppercase

=UPPER(text)

Or

1. On the **Formulas** tab, in the **Function Library** group, click **Text**, and then click **UPPER**.

2. In the **Function Arguments** dialog box, enter or select the source text that you want to convert to uppercase, and then click **OK**.

To convert a text string to lowercase

→ In the cell or formula bar, enter the following formula, where *text* is the source text:

=LOWER(text)

Or

1. On the **Formulas** tab, in the **Function Library** group, click **Text**, and then click **LOWER**.

2. In the **Function Arguments** dialog box, enter or select the source text that you want to convert to lowercase, and then click **OK**.

To capitalize each word of a text string

➡ In the cell or formula bar, enter the following formula, where *text* is the source text:

=*PROPER(text)*

Or

1. On the **Formulas** tab, in the **Function Library** group, click **Text**, and then click **PROPER**.

2. In the **Function Arguments** dialog box, enter or select the source text that you want to convert to lowercase, and then click **OK**.

To join multiple text strings into one cell

➡ In the cell or formula bar, enter the following formula, including up to 255 text strings, which can be in the form of cell references or specific text enclosed in quotation marks:

=*CONCAT(text1,[text2],[text3]...)*

Or

1. On the **Formulas** tab, in the **Function Library** group, click **Text**, and then click **CONCAT**.

2. In the **Function Arguments** dialog box, do the following, and then click **OK**:

   - In the **Text1** box, enter or select the first source text.
   - In the **Text2** box and each subsequent box, enter the additional source text.

4

Objective 4.3 practice tasks

The practice file for these tasks is located in the **MOSExcel2016\Objective4** practice file folder. The folder also contains a result file that you can use to check your work.

➤ Open the **Excel_4-3** workbook, display the **Book List** worksheet, and do the following:

  ❑ In the File By column, create a function that inserts the first letter of the author's last name.

  ❑ In the Locator column, create a function that insert the author's area code (the first three digits of the phone number).

  ❑ In the Biography column, use the CONCAT() function to insert text in the form <u>Joan Lambert is the author of Microsoft Word 2016 Step by Step, which was published by Microsoft Press in 2015.</u> (including the period).

➤ Save the **Excel_4-3** workbook.

➤ Open the **Excel_4-3_results** workbook. Compare the two workbooks to check your work.

➤ Close the open workbooks.

Objective group 5
Create charts and objects

The skills tested in this section of the Microsoft Office Specialist exam for Microsoft Excel 2016 relate to creating charts and objects. Specifically, the following objectives are associated with this set of skills:

5.1 Create charts

5.2 Format charts

5.3 Insert and format objects

You can store a large amount of data in an Excel workbook. When you want to present that data to other people, you might choose to include additional information to help viewers interpret the information, or to present the data in the form of a chart. Using Excel 2016, you can create many types of charts from data stored on one or more worksheets. To simplify the process of choosing a chart type, the Quick Analysis tool recommends charts that are most appropriate for the data you're working with. To aid viewers in interpreting the chart data, you can configure a chart to include identifying elements such as a title, legend, and data markers.

You can enhance the information you present in a workbook by including images such as company logos directly on worksheets, displaying text and graphics in SmartArt business diagrams, and displaying text independent of the worksheet or chart sheet structure within text boxes.

This chapter guides you in studying ways of presenting data in charts and enhancing worksheets by including images, business diagrams, and text boxes.

5

> To complete the practice tasks in this chapter, you need the practice files contained in the **MOSExcel2016\Objective5** practice file folder. For more information, see "Download the practice files" in this book's introduction.

Objective 5.1: Create charts

Charts (also referred to as *graphs*) are created by plotting data points onto a two-dimensional or three-dimensional axis to assist in data analysis and are therefore a common component of certain types of workbooks. Presenting data in the form of a chart can make it easy to identify trends and relationships that might not be obvious from the data itself.

Different types of charts are best suited for different types of data. The following table shows the available chart types and the data they are particularly useful for plotting.

Chart type	Typically used to show	Variations
Area	Multiple data series as cumulative layers showing change over time	Two-dimensional or three-dimensional Independent or stacked data series
Bar	Variations in value over time or the comparative values of several items at a single point in time	Two-dimensional or three-dimensional Stacked or clustered bars Absolute or proportional values
Box & Whisker	Distribution of data within a range, including mean values, quartiles, and outliers	
Column	Variations in value over time or comparisons	Two-dimensional or three-dimensional Stacked or clustered columns Absolute or proportional values
Funnel	Categorized numeric data such as sales or expenses	
Histogram	Frequency of occurrence of values within a data set	Optional Pareto chart includes additive contributions

Chart type	Typically used to show	Variations
Line	Multiple data trends over evenly spaced intervals	Two-dimensional or three-dimensional Independent or stacked lines Absolute or proportional values Can include markers
Pie	Percentages assigned to different components of a single item (nonnegative, nonzero, no more than seven values)	Two-dimensional or three-dimensional Pie or doughnut shape Secondary pie or bar subset
Radar	Percentages assigned to different components of an item, radiating from a center point	Can include markers and fills
Stock	High, low, and closing prices of stock market activity	Can include opening price and volume traded
Sunburst	Comparisons of multilevel hierarchical data	
Surface	Trends in values across two different dimensions in a continuous curve, such as a topographic map	Two-dimensional or three-dimensional Contour or surface area
Treemap	Comparisons of multilevel hierarchical data	
X Y (Scatter)	Relationships between sets of values	Data points as markers or bubbles Optional trendlines
Waterfall	The effect of positive and negative contributions on financial data	Optional connector lines

You can also create combination charts that overlay different data charts in one space.

5

To plot data as a chart, all you have to do is select the data and specify the chart type. You can select any type of chart from the Charts group on the Insert tab. You can also find recommendations based on the selected content either on the Charts tab of the Quick Analysis tool or on the Recommended Charts tab of the Insert Chart dialog box.

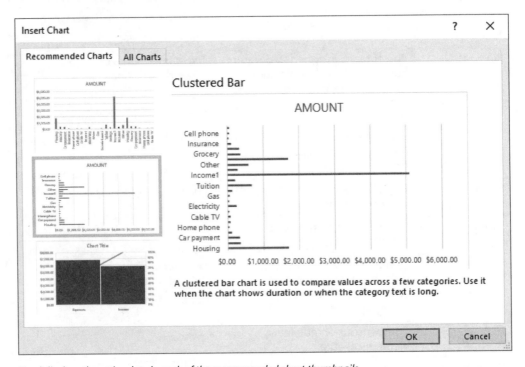

Excel displays the active data in each of the recommended chart thumbnails

---

Tip The Quick Analysis tool provides access to formatting options that pertain to the currently selected data. From the tabs of the Quick Analysis tool, you can apply conditional formatting, perform mathematical operations, create tables and PivotTables, and insert sparklines. Like the Mini Toolbar, the Paste Options menu, and other context-specific tools, the Quick Analysis tool makes existing functionality available in a central location. The reason this is a tool rather than simply a toolbar or menu is that the options shown in the tool—for example, the charts shown on the Charts tab—are selected as appropriate for the current data.

Before you select the data that you want to present as a chart, ensure that the data is correctly set up for the type of chart you want to create (for example, you must set up hierarchical categories differently for a box & whisker, sunburst, or treemap chart than for a bar or column chart). Select only the data you want to appear in the chart. If the data is not in a contiguous range of rows or columns, either rearrange the data or hold down the Ctrl key while you select noncontiguous ranges.

A chart is linked to its worksheet data, so any changes you make to the plotted data are immediately reflected in the chart. If you want to add or delete values in a data series or add or remove an entire series, you need to increase or decrease the range of the plotted data in the worksheet.

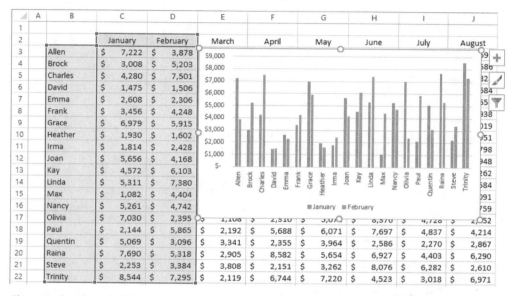

Change a chart by including more or less data

Sometimes a chart does not produce the results you expect because the data series are plotted against the wrong axes; that is, Excel is plotting the data by row when it should be plotting by column, or vice versa. You can quickly switch the rows and columns to see whether that produces the desired effect. You can preview the effect of switching axes in the Change Chart Type dialog box.

You can present a different view of the data in a chart by switching the data series and categories across the axis.

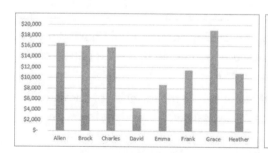
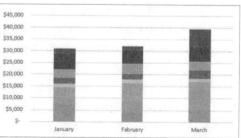

Change a chart by switching the data series and categories

You can swap data across the axis from the Change Chart Type dialog box or you can more precisely control the chart content from the Select Data Source dialog box.

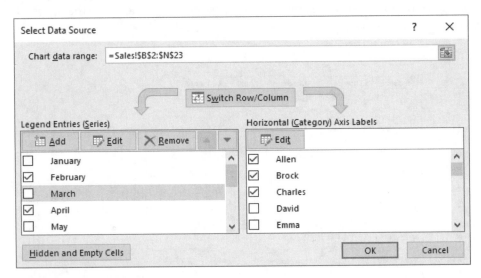

Choosing the data to include in a chart

◇◇

Exam Strategy Practice plotting the same data in different ways. In particular, understand the effects of plotting data by column or by row.

◇◇

To plot data as a chart on the worksheet

1. On the worksheet, select the data that you want to plot in the chart.

2. Do any of the following:

   - On the **Insert** tab, in the **Charts** group, click the general chart type you want, and then on the menu, click the specific chart you want to create.

     ___

     Tip Pointing to a chart type on the menu displays a live preview of the selected data plotted as that chart type.

     ___

   - On the **Insert** tab, in the **Charts** group, click **Recommended Charts**. Preview the recommended charts by clicking the thumbnails in the left pane. Then click the chart type you want, and click **OK**.

   - Click the **Quick Analysis** button that appears in the lower-right corner of the selection, click **Charts**, and then click the chart type you want to create.

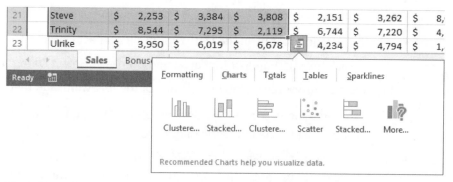

The Quick Analysis menu provides quick access to data transformation options

To modify the data points in a chart

→ In the linked Excel worksheet, change the values within the chart data.

To select the chart data on the linked worksheet

→ Click the chart area or plot area.

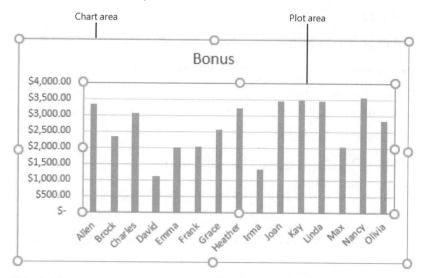

Selecting data on the chart selects the corresponding data on the worksheet

To change the range of plotted data in a selected chart

→ In the linked Excel worksheet, drag the corner handles of the series selectors until they enclose the series you want to plot.

Or

1. Do either of the following:

   - On the **Design** tool tab, in the **Data** group, click **Select Data**.
   - Right-click the chart area or plot area, and then click **Select Data**.

2. In the **Select Data Source** dialog box, do any of the following, and then click **OK**:

   - Click the worksheet icon at the right end of the **Chart data range** box, and then drag to select the full range of data you want to have available.
   - In the **Legend Entries (Series)** list and **Horizontal (Category) Axis Labels** boxes, select the check boxes of the rows and columns of data you want to plot.

To plot additional data series in a selected chart

1. Do either of the following:

   - On the **Design** tool tab, in the **Data** group, click **Select Data**.
   - Right-click the chart area or plot area, and then click **Select Data**.

2. In the **Select Data Source** dialog box, at the top of the **Legend Entries (Series)** list, click **Add**.

3. In the **Edit Series** dialog box, do either of the following:

   - Enter the additional series in the **Series name** box.
   - Click in the **Series name** box and then drag in the worksheet to select the additional series.

4. If necessary, enter or select the series values. Then click **OK**.

5. In the **Select Data Source** dialog box, click **OK**.

To switch the display of a data series in a selected chart between the series axis and the category axis

→ On the **Design** tool tab, in the **Data** group, click the **Switch Row/Column** button.

Or

1. Do either of the following:

   - On the **Design** tool tab, in the **Data** group, click **Select Data**.
   - Right-click the chart area or plot area, and then click **Select Data**.

2. In the **Select Data Source** dialog box, click **Switch Row/Column**, and then click **OK**.

Objective 5.1 practice tasks

The practice file for these tasks is located in the **MOSExcel2016\Objective5** practice file folder. The folder also contains a result file that you can use to check your work.

➤ Open the **Excel_5-1** workbook and do the following:

❑ Plot the data on the **Seattle** worksheet as a 2-D Pie chart on that worksheet.

❑ Plot the data on the **Sales** worksheet as a simple two-dimensional column chart.

➤ On the **Fall Sales** worksheet, do the following:

❑ Switch the rows and columns of the chart.

❑ Change the October sales amount for the Flowers category to 888.25 and ensure that the chart reflects the change.

❑ Expand the data range plotted by the chart to include November, so that you can compare sales for the two months.

➤ Save the **Excel_5-1** workbook.

➤ Open the **Excel_5-1_results** workbook. Compare the two workbooks to check your work.

➤ Close the open workbooks.

✳ Objective 5.2: Format charts

A chart includes many elements, some required and some optional. The chart content can be identified by a *chart title*. Each data series is represented in the chart by a unique color. A *legend* that defines the colors is created by default but is optional. Each data point is represented in the chart by a data marker, and can also be represented by a *data label* that specifies the data point value. The data is plotted against an x-axis (or *category axis*) and a y-axis (or *value axis*). Three-dimensional charts also have a z-axis (or *series axis*). The axes can have titles, and gridlines can more precisely indicate the axis measurements.

To augment the usefulness or the attractiveness of a chart, you can add elements. You can adjust each element in appropriate ways, in addition to adjusting the plot area (the area defined by the axes) and the chart area (the entire chart object). You can move and format most chart elements, and easily add or remove them from the chart.

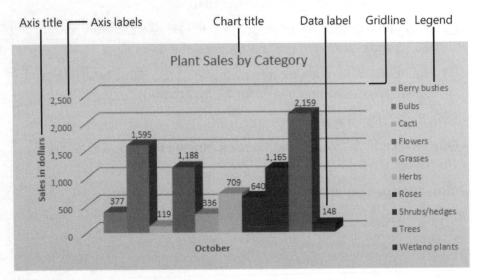

Chart elements can eliminate the need for other explanatory text

---

Tip Data labels can clutter up all but the simplest charts. If you need to show the data for a chart on a separate chart sheet, consider using a data table instead.

You can add and remove chart elements from the Chart Elements pane or from the Design tool tab.

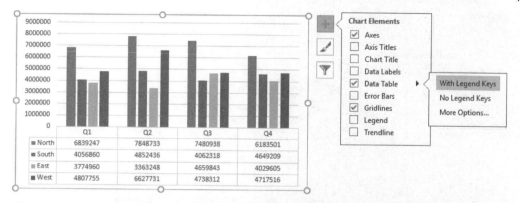

The options in the Chart Elements pane vary based on the chart type

By default, Excel creates charts on the same worksheet as the source data. You can move or size a chart on the worksheet by dragging the chart or its handles, or by specifying a precise position or dimensions. If you prefer to display a chart on its own sheet, you can move it to another worksheet in the workbook, or to a dedicated chart sheet.

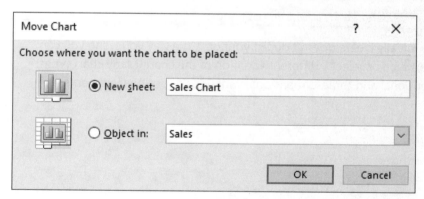

Move a chart to its own sheet to remove the distraction of the background data

You can apply predefined combinations of layouts and styles to quickly format a chart. You can also apply a shape style to the chart area to set it off from the rest of the sheet.

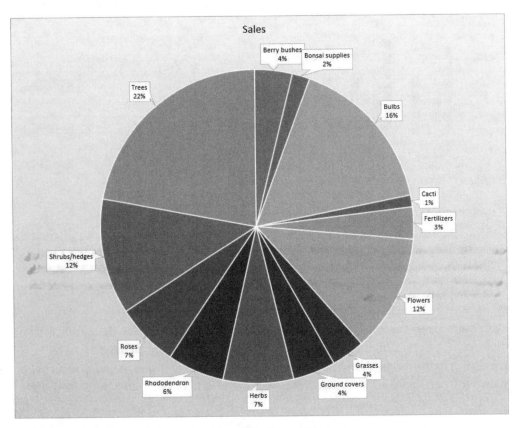

Preset formatting options make it easy to achieve the look you want

If the chart you initially create doesn't depict your data the way you want, you can change the chart type or select a different variation of the chart. Many chart types have two-dimensional and three-dimensional variations or optional elements.

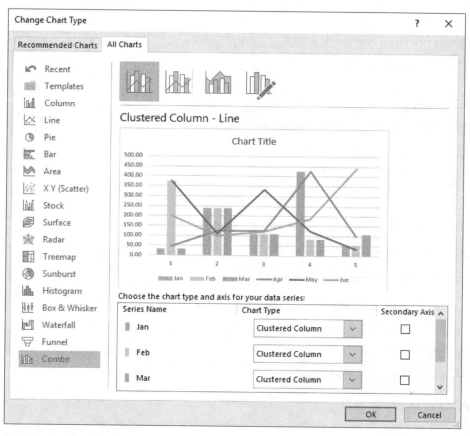

Preview chart data in other types of charts

To display and hide chart elements

→ Click the chart, and then click the **Chart Elements** button (labeled with a plus sign) that appears in the upper-right corner of the chart. In the **Chart Elements** pane, select the check boxes of the elements you want to display, and clear the check boxes of the elements you want to hide.

→ On the **Design** tool tab, in the **Chart Layouts** group, click **Add Chart Element**, click the element type, and then click the specific element you want to display or hide.

→ On the **Design** tool tab, in the **Chart Layouts** group, click **Quick Layout**, and then click the combination of elements you want to display.

5

To resize a chart

→ Select the chart, and then drag the sizing handles.

→ On the **Format** tool tab, in the **Size** group, enter the **Height** and **Width** dimensions.

→ On the **Format** tool tab, click the **Size** dialog box launcher, and enter the **Height** and **Width** dimensions or **Scale Height** and **Scale Width** percentages on the **Size & Properties** page of the **Format Chart Area** pane.

To move a selected chart

→ Drag the chart to another location on the worksheet.

Or

1. On the **Design** tool tab, in the **Location** group, click **Move Chart**.

2. In the **Move Chart** dialog box, select a location and click **OK**.

To change the type of a selected chart

1. On the **Design** tool tab, in the **Type** group, click **Change Chart Type**.

2. In the **Change Chart Type** dialog box, click a new type and sub-type, and then click **OK**.

To apply a style to a selected chart

→ On the **Design** tool tab, in the **Chart Styles** gallery, click the style you want.

→ Click the **Chart Styles** button (labeled with a paintbrush) that appears in the upper-right corner of the chart. On the **Style** page of the **Chart Styles** pane, click the style you want.

To apply a shape style to a selected chart

→ On the **Format** tool tab, in the **Shape Styles** gallery, click the style you want.

To change the color scheme of a selected chart

→ On the **Design** tool tab, in the **Chart Styles** group, click **Change Colors**, and then click the color scheme you want.

→ Click the **Chart Styles** button that appears in the upper-right corner of the chart. On the **Color** page of the **Chart Styles** pane, click the color scheme you want.

→ Apply a different theme to the workbook.

> **See Also** For information about applying themes, see "Objective 1.3: Format work-
> sheets and workbooks."

Objective 5.2 practice tasks

The practice files for these tasks are located in the **MOSExcel2016\\Objective5** practice file folder. The folder also contains a result file that you can use to check your work.

➤ Open the **Excel_5-2** workbook, display the **Sales** worksheet, and do the following:

❑ Change the pie chart to a 3-D Clustered Column chart.

❑ Apply *Layout 1, Style 7* to the chart.

❑ Apply the *Subtle Effect – Olive Green, Accent 3* shape style.

❑ Increase the size of the chart until it occupies cells A1:L23.

❑ Move the chart to a new chart sheet named <u>Sales Chart</u>.

➤ On the **Seattle** worksheet, do the following:

❑ Add the title <u>Air Quality Index Report</u> to the chart.

❑ Add data labels that show the percentage of the whole that is represented by each data marker.

➤ Save the **Excel_5-2** workbook.

➤ Open the **Excel_5-2_results** workbook. Compare the two workbooks to check your work.

➤ Close the open workbooks.

Objective 5.3: Insert and format objects

Although graphics are not frequently associated with the storage of data within Excel workbooks, it is worthwhile to note that when preparing to present data, you can incorporate almost all of the graphic elements available in Microsoft Word and PowerPoint into an Excel workbook. This can be particularly useful when creating summary pages or when a workbook must provide a standalone information source for text content in addition to data.

Tip You use the same methods to insert and format graphic objects in Excel as you do in other Microsoft Office programs. As an experienced Excel user, you are likely familiar with the methods for inserting, creating, and configuring graphic objects in other programs.

Insert text boxes and shapes

To convey information more succinctly, you can add text. When you add text directly to a worksheet, you are restricted by the width and height of the worksheet cells in which you must insert the text. To bypass that restriction or to distinctly separate the text from the worksheet data, you can insert the text in a text box or shape that you can position independently on the worksheet. You can also use shapes as simple navigational aids that use hyperlinks to move to a specific location.

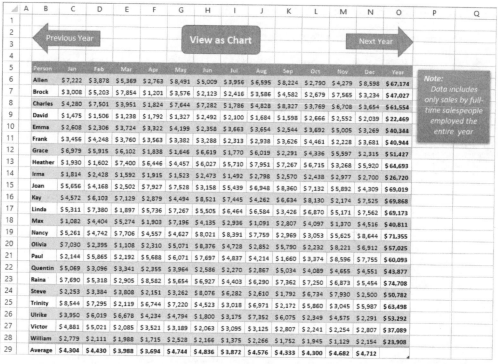

Text within a text box or shape is independent of the worksheet content

Shapes can be simple, such as lines, circles, or squares; or more complex, such as stars, hearts, and arrows. You can enter text inside a shape, and apply formatting effects to both the shape and the text. You format both text boxes and shapes by using commands on the Format tool tab for Drawing Tools.

Easily apply formatting that matches the color scheme of other workbook elements

To insert a text box on a worksheet

1. On the **Insert** tab, in the **Text** group, click **Text Box**.

2. In the worksheet, click to insert a small (one character) text box that expands when you enter text, or drag to draw the text box the size that you want.

3. Enter or paste the text you want to display in the text box.

To draw a shape

1. On the **Insert** tab, in the **Illustrations** group, click the **Shapes** button.

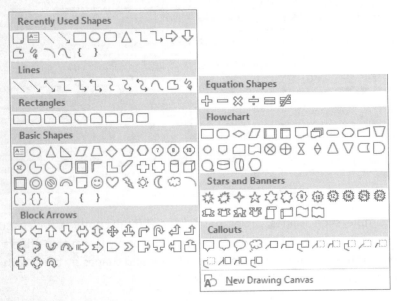

More than 150 shapes are available as starting points for a custom shape

2. In the **Shapes** gallery, click the shape you want, and then do one of the following:

   - Click anywhere on the page to insert a standard-size shape.

   - Drag anywhere on the page to draw a shape of the size and aspect ratio that you want.

   Tip To draw a shape with a 1:1 aspect ratio (equal height and width), hold down the Shift key while dragging.

To add text to a shape

➔ Click the shape to select it, and then enter the text.

➔ Right-click the shape, click **Add Text** or **Edit Text**, and then enter the text.

To format a selected text box or shape

➔ To change the shape, on the **Format** tool tab, in the **Insert Shapes** group, click **Edit Shape**, click **Change Shape**, and then click the shape you want.

➔ To change the shape fill, outline, or effects, on the **Format** tool tab, use the formatting options in the **Shape Styles** group.

➔ To rotate the shape, on the **Format** tool tab, in the **Arrange** group, click **Rotate Objects**, and then click the rotation option you want.

To resize a text box or shape

➔ Click the text box or shape to select it, and then do any of the following:

- Drag the top or bottom sizing handle to change the height.
- Drag the left or right sizing handle to change the width.
- Drag a corner sizing handle to change the width and height and maintain the aspect ratio.
- On the **Format** tool tab, in the **Size** group, enter or select the **Height** and **Width** dimensions.
- On the **Format** tool tab, in the **Size** group, click the dialog box launcher. In the **Format** *Object* dialog box that opens, select the **Lock aspect ratio** check box if you want to maintain the aspect ratio, and then enter or select the height or width.

To format text in a text box or shape

➔ Select the text box or shape. On the **Format** tool tab, use the formatting options in the **WordArt Styles** group.

➔ Select the text, and then use the formatting options on the **Mini Toolbar** or in the **Font** group on the **Home** tab.

5

Insert images

You can enhance workbook content by adding an image, perhaps a company logo, a product image, or an image that represents the concept you want to convey to the workbook viewer.

Add a product image to a worksheet that you will use as a catalog page

After you insert an image in a document, you can modify it in many ways. For example, you can crop or resize a picture, change the picture's brightness and contrast, recolor it, apply artistic effects to it, and compress it to reduce the size of the document containing it. You can apply a wide range of preformatted styles to a picture to change its shape and orientation, in addition to adding borders and picture effects.

You format images by using commands on the Format tool tab for Pictures.

You can format an image in Excel in the same ways that you do in PowerPoint or Word

To insert a picture on a worksheet

1. On the **Insert** tab, in the **Illustrations** group, click the **Pictures** button.

2. In the **Insert Picture** dialog box, browse to and click the file you want. Then do one of the following:

   - Click **Insert** to insert the picture into the worksheet.

   - In the **Insert** list, click **Link to File** to insert a picture that will update automatically if the picture file changes.

   - In the **Insert** list, click **Insert and Link** to insert a picture that you can manually update if the picture file changes.

To apply artistic effects to a selected picture on a worksheet

→ On the **Format** tool tab, in the **Adjust** group, click **Artistic Effects**, and then in the gallery, click the effect you want to apply.

To apply a style to a selected picture on a worksheet

→ On the **Format** tool tab, in the **Picture Styles** group, expand the **Quick Styles** gallery, and then click the style you want to apply.

Or

1. On the **Format** tool tab, click the **Picture Styles** dialog box launcher.

2. In the **Format Picture** pane, on the **Fill & Line** and **Effects** pages, choose the options that you want to apply.

To change the size and/or shape of a selected picture on a worksheet

→ Drag its sizing handles.

→ On the **Format** tool tab, in the **Size** group, change the **Height** and **Width** settings.

→ On the **Format** tool tab, click the **Size** dialog box launcher. Then on the **Size & Properties** page of the **Format Picture** pane, change the **Height**, **Width**, and **Scale** settings.

To move a picture on a worksheet

→ Drag the picture to a new location.

5

To copy a picture to a new location on a worksheet

→ Hold down the **Ctrl** key and drag the picture to the second location.

To format a selected picture

→ Use the commands in the **Adjust** group on the **Format** tool tab to remove the picture background; adjust the sharpness, brightness, and contrast; apply artistic effects; and compress the picture to minimize the file size.

→ Use the commands in the **Picture Styles** group on the **Format** tool tab to apply preconfigured combinations of effects or to apply a border, shadow, reflection, glow, soft edge, beveled edge, or three-dimensional effect.

→ Use the commands in the **Arrange** group on the **Format** tool tab to control the relationship of the picture to the sheet and to other pictures on the sheet, and to rotate or flip the picture.

→ Use the commands in the **Size** group on the **Format** tool tab to change the picture height and width and to crop the picture manually, to a specific aspect ratio, to a shape, or to fill or fit a specific space.

Provide alternative text for accessibility

Alternative text (also referred to as *alt text*) is descriptive text assigned to an Excel table, chart, image, or other object that either might not show up correctly on the page or might not be available to screen reading software. The alternative text provides readers with information about the object content or purpose. In a PDF file, for example, if your content includes alternative text, a reader can point to an image on the screen to display a description of the image.

You assign alternative text to an object as an object property. You can assign both a title and a description to an image.

To add alternative text to an object

1. Do one of the following:

   • Right-click the chart area of a chart, and then click **Format Chart Area**.

   • Right-click a text box or shape, and then click **Format Shape**.

   • Right-click an image, and then click **Format Picture**.

2. In the **Format *Object*** pane, click the **Size & Properties** button, and then click the **Alt Text** heading to display the input boxes, if they aren't already visible.

3. In the **Title** box, enter a short title for the object. People who use screen reading software will hear the title first and can then choose whether to have the description read.

4. In the **Description** box, enter a description that provides the information you intend for a reader to get from looking at the object.

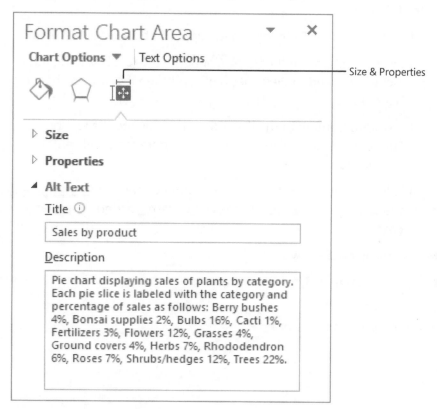

Alt text provides a text description of a visual object

Excel saves your changes in the object properties.

Objective 5.3 practice tasks

The practice file for these tasks is located in the **MOSExcel2016\Objective5** practice file folder. The folder also contains a result file that you can use to check your work.

➤ Open the **Excel_5-3a** workbook, display the **Summary** sheet, and do the following:

❑ Insert the **Excel_5-3b** logo in the upper-left corner of the sheet.

❑ Insert a text box on the sheet. Configure the text box to be three inches wide and three inches high, and align it below the heading "Our Prediction."

❑ Insert the content of the **Excel_5-3c** text file into the text box. Format the text in 20-point orange Candara font, and center it in the text box.

❑ Add alternative text to the logo, using the title <u>Company logo</u> and the description <u>Cartoon image of a person wearing an airplane costume.</u>

➤ Save the **Excel_5-3a** workbook.

➤ Open the **Excel_5-3_results** workbook. Compare the two workbooks to check your work.

➤ Close the open workbooks.

Index

About the author

JOAN LAMBERT has worked closely with Microsoft technologies since 1986, and in the training and certification industry since 1997. As President and CEO of Online Training Solutions, Inc. (OTSI), Joan guides the translation of technical information and requirements into useful, relevant, and measurable resources for people who are seeking certification of their computer skills or who simply want to know how to get things done efficiently.

Joan is the author or coauthor of more than four dozen books about Windows and Office (for Windows, Mac, and iPad), five generations of Microsoft Office Specialist certification study guides, video-based training courses for SharePoint and OneNote, QuickStudy guides for Windows and Office, and the GO! series book for Outlook 2016.

Blissfully based in America's Finest City, Joan is a Microsoft Certified Professional, Microsoft Office Specialist Master (for all versions of Office since Office 2003), Microsoft Certified Technology Specialist (for Windows and Windows Server), Microsoft Certified Technology Associate (for Windows), Microsoft Dynamics Specialist, and Microsoft Certified Trainer.

ONLINE TRAINING SOLUTIONS, INC. (OTSI) specializes in the design and creation of Microsoft Office, SharePoint, and Windows training solutions and the production of online and printed training resources. For more information about OTSI, visit *www.otsi.com,* or for advance information about upcoming training resources and informative tidbits about technology and publishing, follow us on Facebook at *www.facebook.com/Online.Training.Solutions.Inc.*

Acknowledgments

I am extremely grateful for the unflagging support and contributions of Jaime Odell, Kathy Krause, and Susie Carr at OTSI—this book (and so many others) wouldn't exist without our fabulous team! Thank you also to Rosemary Caperton and Kim Spilker at Microsoft Press, and Laura Norman at Pearson Education, for making the MOS Study Guide series for Office 2016 a reality.

Finally, I am so very grateful for the support of my daughter, Trinity. Her confidence, encouragement, and terrific cooking when I'm working late bring me great joy.

Now that you've read the book...

Tell us what you think!

Was it useful?
Did it teach you what you wanted to learn?
Was there room for improvement?

Let us know at https://aka.ms/tellpress

Your feedback goes directly to the staff at Microsoft Press,
and we read every one of your responses. Thanks in advance!

 Microsoft